Parables from (a not quite) Paradise, NV 89154

V. 1 The Nevada Public Radio Commentaries

By

William N. Thompson

1st Books Library
Bloomington, IN
2003

ISBN: 1-4107-1954-5 (e-book)
ISBN: 1-4107-1955-3 (Paperback)

Library of Congress Control Number: 2003091082

This book is printed on acid free paper.

Printed in the United States of America
Bloomington, IN

Cover Photo by Steve Marcus
(with permission)

1stBooks - rev. 05/10/03

Preface

In a city where the mainstream media are slow to criticize the one horse in a one horse town, Bill Thompson is a breath of dry scratchy desert air. His deep understanding of the gaming industry informs many of his essays, But I'm happy to have him wander off topic now and then in his radio commentaries. Then I hold my own breath and open my email account the next day and wait for comments and messages. To say he's a lightning rod is perhaps an overstatement,

Florence Rogers of KNPR

but in Nevada critical thinking about our woeful record on social services, equitable taxes and education is a precious commodity indeed. I know we're on the right track when highly placed casino executives call for him to be taken off the air.

I'm very proud to have carved out airtime for Bill's essays on the airwaves of Nevada Public Radio and I hope they read as well on the page as they do in Bill's prosecutorial voice—you'll have to imagine the contrast between NPR's Bob Edwards soothing enunciation and Bill's urgent appeals for commonsense in our "Battleborn" Silver State.

KNPR Studios, Las Vegas

What our listeners rarely hear is Bill's infectious chuckle and the glee with which he constructs his arguments, also the many hours he's spent with me as a newcomer to Nevada, attempting to lasso the ways our one horse town, Las Vegas. For that I am grateful.

Florence Rogers
Director of Programming and
Assistant General Manager
Nevada Public Radio

Contents

Introduction

Parables from (a not quite) Paradise, NV 89154 offers thirty essays, twenty-five of which appeared as commentaries on KNPR (Nevada Public Radio in Las Vegas) from mid-2001 through the end of 2002. In May 2001, Florence Rogers, Program Director of KNPR, was seeking voices to offer commentaries on public issues and topics of general interest to southern Nevadans. A friend of mine, Adam Carriere, weekend host of the radio station, suggested that I might be one such voice. Adam and I have participated each year in the Far West and American Popular Culture conferences sponsored by Professor Felicia Campbell of the English Department at the University of Nevada, Las Vegas. There I rant and rave about things political and things related to life in Las Vegas. I suspect that I irritate as much as I entertain, but then maybe I entertained Adam, as his conference presentations entertained me. Florence Rogers gave me a call, and I started talking. She has called back many times again so I guess I have been more than just irritating. Nonetheless, I do hope my essays occasionally irritate and arouse ire and even emotions.

I have kept the essays fairly close to the way they were presented on the air. However, I have rearranged their order so as to keep commentaries on the same or related topics next to one another (ergo, gambling or legislative politics and taxation). At the end of each of these essays, I indicate the first date it appeared on KNPR.

I am a critic and oftentimes I sense that I am a cynic. I do push political viewpoints, but I believe that my views cross political party lines. I am a registered Democrat, but twenty five years ago I was elected to office (supervisor of Kalamazoo Township, Michigan) on the Republican ticket. I have split my ballot almost every time since the 1960s when I started voting. I have a tendency to vote against incumbents as I subscribe to the Jacksonian philosophy of "rotation of office holders." I also support Jeffersonian notions such as small government and individual responsibility. But then, I can be inconsistent in applying any philosophy, and also inconsistent over time. Consistency in a changing environment is not always a virtue.

Democracy demands both a degree of participation and loyalty (even emotional or "blind" loyalty) from citizens. These essays represent my most overt political activity over the past two years. Yet they also are an exercise in my loyalty to the American political system. I choose to start the collection with a statement of loyalty. I follow with a consideration of world peace and the lessons we can learn from the amazing sloth, an animal I met in the jungles of the Peruvian Amazon.

Most of the essays in this volume—the first 25—do appear on the KNPR website: www.knpr.org/commentary. A second volume will consist of essays on more national and international topics written for the History News Network (www.historynewsnetwork.org), edited by Richard Shenkman. Chapters 26 and 27 present a preview to that volume with two essays from HNN on the topic of nuclear waste disposal, both a national and also very much a local Nevada issue and concern.

These are followed by two essays based upon presentations I have made elsewhere. Chapter 28 records views I gave to the Nevada Gaming Commission on something the continues to raise my ire—slot machines in our grocery stores. Chapter 29 then presents what I consider to be the one factor most responsible for our economic success in Nevada—I call it "the Win Win Game." The final chapter is an essay that I wrote two decades ago. The essay on my initial years in Las Vegas (1980-1981) was published as "How I Became a Native" in a book edited by University of Nevada, Las Vegas History Professor Hal Rothman and Mike Davis, a Professor of History at the State University of New York, Stony Brook. The book, The Grit Beneath the Glitter: Tales from the Real Las Vegas, was published by the University of California Press (2002). The Press graciously gave permission, for which I give appreciation, for it to be reprinted in this volume.

The writer offers appreciation to others who have assisted in this effort. To Flo, Adam, and Richard—who launched the essays. To fellow faculty and staff members of my university who gave comments on my ideas, to the members of the news media who have called me time and again to ask questions, but who always end up giving me more information than they get. I am especially thankful for staff members who have kept the words flowing in a mechanical but essential manner. Thanks are due Bob Potts of the UNLV Center for Business and Economic Research who rescued the manuscript from my computer just before it crashed. He saved the files and formatted them so they could be sent to the publisher. Mary Riddel of the Center offered valuable critiques and also a photograph of Alf which is used in Chapter 14. I thank Diana Sjoberg for the author's photograph at the end of the book, Steve Marcus for the cover photograph, and David Schwartz and Peter Michel of Special Collections of the University for Nevada, Las Vegas Library for permission to use photographs from their files. My thanks also go to Vid Beldavs, Elizabeth Cole, and the staff of 1st Books Library for bringing it all together.

The reader will note that the writer does not really reside in "Las Vegas" as such, but rather in "Paradise Valley" a planning district that is within the political jurisdiction served by the Clark County government—not the city of Las Vegas government. So therefore, one should not in derision suggest he teaches at "Tumbleweed Tech," or the "University of Maryland...Parkway," or the "University of Never Leaving Vegas." On the other hand, perhaps he doesn't really teach at "UNLV," but instead, "UNPV."

Chapter 1. Red, White and Blue: Long May It Wave

People of the world vote with their feet. They choose to come to America more than anywhere else. They think there are good things about America. We have a day to celebrate the good things about America. We should.

The 1975 film "Nashville," featured the song "We Must Be Doing Something Right to Last 200 Years." Although a terrible song, its message deserves reflection. May I suggest a revised title, "We Must Be Doing Something Right to Last 225 Years?" On this July 4th we should identify things that we as a nation are doing right.

My son Tim met Carmenza Cespedes while the two served in the Peace Corps in Changinola, Bocas del Toro Province, Panama. Carmenza's mother came to Queens, New York from Colombia. She thinks America is doing something right. She says: "No matter who you are, rich or poor, black or white, you go to a grocery store you stand in line, the first in line gets served first, no matter who you are."

Roy Kawaguchi appreciates that our liberties allow people to think and to express their thoughts—and others respect them even if they disagree. He came to Las Vegas seeking opportunities in tourism. He is happy that America has given him choices he would not have elsewhere.

Many pursue business choices for wealth, but not a selfish wealth. The quest to gain helps all because of something derided as "trickle down." But it is not that. It is a cascade as if a meteorite shower bringing increased value to society. With this spread of wealth all can be winners.

With possessions people have control over destinies, and so here masses feel good about themselves and good about life. Love of self is part of America. It is not bad.

With self respect and self love, we gain an inner sense that allows good feelings about others, love for others, a desire to help others.

Americans give of their time, their wealth, and even of their lives to help others.

In 1862 at the age of 29 my great great uncle Richard Thompson left his family to join Illinois Volunteers and march to Tennessee to end slavery. He fell at Nashville. In 1967 when called, twenty-three year old Ronald Colwell of Samaria, Michigan answered and embraced Army life becoming an officer before he left for southeast Asia, before he gave everything.

Bob Bush gave in Viet Nam and he came back. He decided he should not stop giving. He is a builder in Las Vegas, but he has spent much time with Habitat for Humanity. Debbie Bush's family came from Mexico. She has one job for pay, but many jobs with love for others in the Family Assistance Center of University Church and with the Boys and Girls Clubs. She recruits volunteers. If you have a hand to offer, just hit www.debbiebush.com.

Those who give take risks. Risk taking is endemic with Americans; that makes Las Vegas part of the spirit of America, so much so that we are called All American City by Time and Newsweek magazines. Here and across our land people risk for changes to be better, and they encourage their country to change to be better.

We are a nation of nations, but not just a melting pot, we are a mosaic. In other countries people from elsewhere like the Cespedes family would be Colombian. Roy Kawaguchi would be Japanese. Debbie Bush Hispanic. Here they are that but they are Americans too.

Twenty-five years ago, in 1976, July 4th fell on Sunday. I attended Westwood Church in Kalamazoo, Michigan. We did not sing God Bless America or the Star Spangled Banner—maybe pastor Alan McCreedy didn't relished lines about bombs bursting in air. We sang "Finlandia." I was disappointed. But maybe Finlandia is a good song to sing on July 4.

It tells of a beautiful land with blue skies and wonderful people who love their land; but then it also tells that other countries are beautiful, and that other people love their lands too. Americans see beauty in entire world, and in wonderful peoples from other places who love their lands still, even though they came to America for respect, freedom, choices, the opportunity to be better, and opportunity to do better for others.

We've lasted 225 years. We are doing many things right. Does this mean we are perfect? It's July 4, you're damn right we're perfect!
—July 4, 2001

Chapter 2. Everything I Need to Know About World Peace, I Learned from the Sloth

In July I toured Peru with a group of Nevada school teachers. We saw ancient Cuzco and exotic Machu Picchu, and we visited villages in the Amazon jungle. My final days were in the capital of Lima. It is always refreshing to escape CNN and Fox News and stories of world strife for a couple weeks. But then Lima did bring reality back to us with its brutal traffic and gridlock at each intersection, its unchecked pollution and gripping poverty. But without television we heard nothing of Afghanistan, Palestine, Israel, Pakistan, India or Iraq. Almost heaven.

Was I in Nirvana? Perhaps I was close. Not in Lima, but maybe in the jungle.

Western society embraces an ethic of progress. The ethic is reflected in the biblical admonition that mankind should go forth and subdue the land. An individualism supported in religion is often a playing out of a win-lose game of social Darwinism. Militarism is a natural concomitant our values. Yet Western religions also envision a quite different Nirvanic "pot of gold," at the end of the rainbow we call life. In contrast with the images of CNN and the street scenes of Lima, the heaven we seem to wish to seek is one of satisfaction, relaxation, non-competition, non-acquisition, and above all, PEACE.

In the Amazon jungle I sensed that a Nirvana of peace was alive on Earth. There we spotted among the leaves of a Kapok tree, a three-toed sloth. Here was a peaceful creature.

The sloth is not a taker. The eight pound mammal does not engage in any win-lose or parasitic games. As the sloth survives, it harms no other living creature. The sloth eats only leaves, deriving both nutritional substance and water needs from foliage. Yet the sloth gives back to the trees and to other creatures as well. He exists in a symbiotic and synergistic relationship with all others in the environment.

The sloth's hairy body is a breeding ground for the algae of the region. The algae in turn give the body of the sloth a greenish coloring pattern that affords it a camouflaged hiding from predators. While the sloth spends most of its time hanging in sleep in mid level

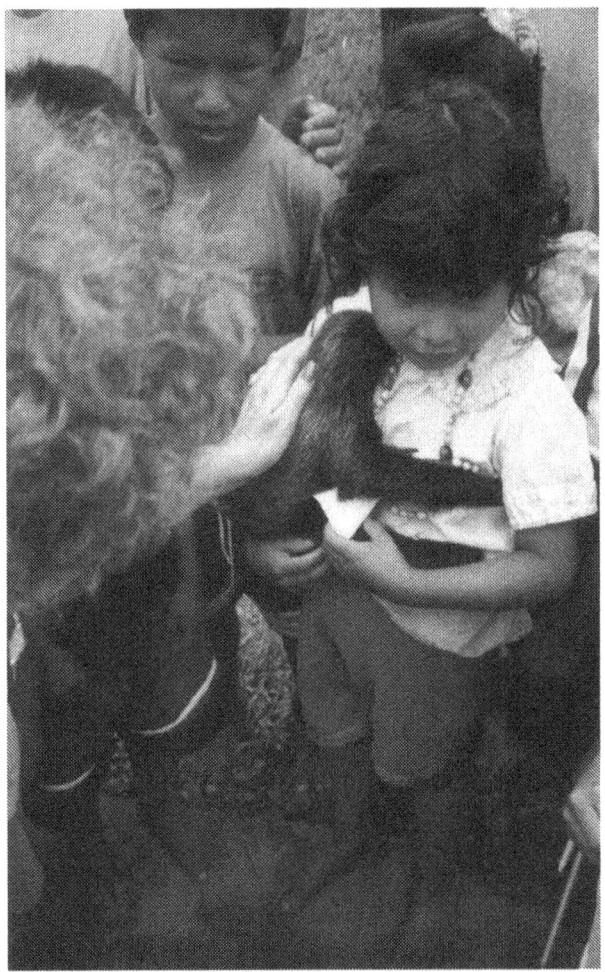

Girl holds sloth in village near Amazon jungle.

branches of its trees, it does seek energy from the sun by rising to higher limbs. The sunshine, in turn, gives valuable heat to the algae as well, helping sustain their growth.

The long stringing hair of the sloth is also the residential home of a special sloth moth. With its limited dietary needs (the sloth craves only what it needs, unlike human beings, not what it wants), the sloth needs to discard wastes only once a week. In the process of doing so, it descends the tree, very slowly, digs a hole, deposits the waste and in an environmentally correct nice manner covers up the hole when it is done. However as the waste is being deposited, the sloth moth also deposits eggs in the material. The burial then protects the eggs. As the eggs are now nurtured, the soils about the waste have also been enriched by it, and so are able to feed the tree that gives the sloth its home and its very limited food supply.

The sloth is very vulnerable to the animals which prey upon it, notably the harpy eagle and the jaguar. The sloth has sharp claws which can be used in defense. They are never used as offensive weapons. The animal's greatest protection comes from its ability to hide. The acts of stealth are aided by the camouflage coloring and also by the sloth's ability to remain still for hours and hours at a time. The animal sleeps in an upside down position hanging from limbs of the tree for as many as 20 hours every day.

The sloth is in its most dangerous position when it descends the tree to do its weekly duty. It is the slowest of all mammals. Its legs cannot move it, instead it pulls itself along the ground at a rate of a few feet per hour. On the other hand, the long arms of the sloth enable the animal to swim with great ability, especially with a speed that can take the sloth away from pursuing jaguars.

The animal's weakness inclines it toward an complete aversion to any conflict within its own population. The sloth will inhabit only a few trees during its lifetime. It will bond with these trees and mark them with its individual smells. The others of the species will respect its trees, and in turn the sloth is not at all motivated to seek out trees belonging to others of its kind.

The sloths are solitary creatures that spend almost their entire lifetimes alone in the midst of their individual trees. The concept of group based battles is totally out of the realm of contemplation for these animals.

Males and females get along very well. Males and females meet for only three days a year. It takes the animals three days to engage in the mating act. After the three days the male retreats to his tree, dreaming about the moment during his long episodes of sleep. Well, of course, the female is left with a burden, but it is not overwhelming. A period of gestation lasts six months, and most of this time the female is sleeping and just hanging around her tree. After birth, the young sloth clings to the mother for about two months, observing the slow cycle of activity. It is then taken to a tree of its own and released.

The female then, like the male, can enjoy four to five months of solitude.

In the lexicon of man, the sloth has been much abused. Religions that seek peace have overlooked this specie's almost unique contribution. Instead, the sloth has been set forth as a model for one of the seven deadly sins—laziness. This is unkind, and unjustified. When we go to sleep, we pray for peace. We envision a heaven that is much like the peaceful world of the sloth. Lazy? What do we think of all day—ways to take advantage of others and then ways to avoid conflict with others. The sloth probably dreams our dreams as well, wakes up, looks around, and sees that indeed, the dreamed-of Nirvana is at hand. So it goes back to sleep. Why not?

The central prophet and creative spirit of the most prominent religion of the Western World offered the words that should elevate the sloth to a position if not of worship itself, at least of emulation, "It is more blessed to give..." World peace could be at hand. If only mankind could be more like the sloth.

— September 3, 2002

Chapter 3. Two Sides to the Nevada Coin

Nevadans will soon be able to celebrate as the U.S. Mint will issue a 25-cent coin commemorating the state of Nevada as part of our federal Union.

But what should be on the two faces of the coin?

I might suggest dark humor—a mushroom cloud, a caricature of Joe Conforte and his Mustang Ranch, an Elvis Wedding chapel. With a bit more seriousness, we could feature industry figures and a clock showing dice for hour numbers. Profiles of Bugsy Siegel, Lansky, Hughes, or the latter day Wynn and Adelson could be on the coin. I won't make such suggestions. I will be very serious. Our state has very serious things to celebrate.

We are the Battleborn State. Among all the others, we were given statehood in order to preserve our national Union at a time of Civil War. Our admission was also critical for adoption of the 13th Amendment which ended slavery. We must celebrate the fact that the existence of Nevada means national union and freedom. Events from the 1860s should be placed on one side of the new coin.

On the other side we should recognize a recent event that still cries out for a celebration never held.

While some may find it parochial or regional, the whole state should now celebrate the accomplishment of the 1990 UNLV Running Rebels basketball team led by coach Jerry Tarkanian and his all American players.

It is funny that any small Iowa farm town will have a sign at its borders proclaiming that its high school girls' softball team won the class C regional title in 1983.

However, interpersonal battles between a university president and coach stopped us from having a celebration after a 1990 victory unmatched in American college sports history. Nowhere in Las Vegas is there a publicly visible sign simply saying we won the national basketball championship. Not on campus, not even outside of our arena.

Instead of savoring the moment, we heard one of the great non-sequiturs of all time. We were told that UNLV would not be canceling classes to enjoy the merriment of victory, because UNLV was "a great academic institution." We retrenched and held a singular rally, shouting but one word—"Repeat." Ergo, we stood as if we were losers and cried out "Wait until next year."

It was to be a futile exercise, next year did not come. Oh, we came so close, but we did not "repeat." So again we retreated, and our retreating posture is still much in evidence today, as our university displays a monumental inferiority complex in both its academic and athletic sectors. While we wait for the illusive "next year," we go about our tasks as if we are losers. We need to break this cycle, we need a celebration. What we accomplished in the sports world was so big that we must celebrate. If we never do, we will always cling to the notion that we are losers.

Rebel Super Fan Craig Kenny at the Final Four Tourney in Indianapolis – We failed to 'Repeat'.

But we are not losers. We helped win a civil war that restored national unity. We achieve the victory that ended slavery. We won freedom. Our state is a state of victories. Our state is a state of champions. Let us celebrate victories and champions on our new national coin.

—February 22, 2002

Chapter 4. Why Jerry Tarkanian is My Favorite Basketball Coach of All Time

Ah. March Madness is over for 2002. Alas, it is the University of Maryland not the University of Maryland Parkway that waves the champion's banner. But March Madness did bring a measure of gladness along with sadness to southern Nevada. Our Men's and Women's teams at UNLV did well toward the end, both closing their seasons in national tournaments. And we do rejoice that Indiana beat Duke—some feelings will never die.

However, we must sadly realize that "The Greatest" has retired from the basketball coaching ranks. Jerry Tarkanian is my favorite basketball coach of all time. Let me tell you why.

It was February 4, 1989. The UC-Irvine fans were watching their "Anteater" basketball team play brilliantly against the favored squad from Las Vegas, the nation's sixteenth-ranked team, the UNLV Running Rebels coached by legendary Jerry Tarkanian. The teams exchanged leads several times, but still the Anteaters looked almost dominating as they raced to a nine-point second half lead. Yet the Rebels kept coming back and the game was going down to the wire. In the last seconds, Irvine's Jeff Herdman was fouled and he had a chance to put the game away. However, he made only one shot, and with ten seconds left, Irvine led 99-96.

The Rebels could tie. The ball was inbounded to Greg Anthony. Out of the corner of his eye, he saw Anderson Hunt open across the floor. Anthony heaved a long pass to the speedy Hunt. Hunt dribbled the ball past the Anteater defenders. He dashed past the three point arc, went straight to the hoop, and laid the ball in. Two points. Irvine took the ball, inbounded it, and time ran out. The game was over. The Irvine Anteaters 99, the UNLV Running Rebels 98.

I was watching the game on my living room television in Las Vegas. I was stunned. We needed a three-point shot to take the game into overtime. We went for a two-point shot. Incredible. I couldn't believe it, but there it was on instant replay. A two-point shot. The announcer paused for a commercial break after saying he was going to get coach Tarkanian to the microphone in a second.

This was going to be good. How does the winningest college basketball coach of all time explain this one? How does any coach react to such a foolish play?

Soon the anxious announcer was eagerly shoving the microphone into the coach's face. "Coach, what's your reaction to that final..." Tarkanian cut off the announcer, saying, "First, I want to congratulate my good friend coach Bill Mulligan. His Irvine team played a great game, he outcoached me, they deserve their victory."

The announcer tried again, "But coach, could you comment on that last..." Again Tarkanian interrupted the announcer. "Second," he said. "I want to congratulate my team. They played awfully hard tonight. They got behind but they never quit. I am really proud of our effort, a coach can't ask for anything more than we gave on the floor tonight."

Finally, the announcer got his question in, "What about that young freshman Hunt's drive on the last play?" Tarkanian held up his hand, and responded. "Anderson played very hard tonight. I am very proud of his effort. Anderson Hunt is a great player. Anderson Hunt is going to win a lot of games for UNLV."

I sighed. This is not what I expected to hear out of the coach's mouth. But this was the response that came from one of the greatest coaches of all time. This response is why he was one of the greatest coaches of all time.

So much of life is controlled by self-fulfilling prophesies. And so it came to be. In the NCAA tournament that year, UNLV faced the number one team Arizona in the West Region. It was only seven weeks after the Irvine game. The Rebels were down by two points to the heavily favored Wildcats, with under five seconds to go. Again Anderson Hunt got the ball, stopping outside the arc, he fired up a three-point shot at the buzzer. The announcer screamed, "It's in. 68-67. The Rebels have defeated the number one team in the country."

The team was even stronger in 1990. They made it to the Final Four. In their victorious semifinal game against Georgia Tech, Anderson Hunt scored 20 points. In the final victory over Duke, a victory that brought a national championship trophy to Las Vegas, Hunt scored 29 points. He was named the most valuable player in the Final Four national tourney.

Coach Tarkanian at McNichols Arena Denver where he leads the Rebels to a National Championship.

Unceasing support and praise for his players, confidence in his players, and loyalty to his players. These have been the hallmarks of Jerry Tarkanian's coaching career. On February 4, 1989, I witnessed an exhibition in coaching greatness. That is when I decided that Jerry Tarkanian was my favorite basketball coach of all time.
—April 10, 2002

Chapter 5. Let's Put Yucca Mountain in Context

I have a friend. His name is Sisyphus. He's the one who tries to push a rock up over a mountain. But just as he reaches the peak, the rock slips out of his hands and rolls back down. And so he has to try again, always with the same results, over and over again. So it is that the leaders of Nevada seem to be fighting the establishment of a high level nuclear waste repository at Yucca Mountain 70 miles from Las Vegas. No matter how hard they fight, the rock keeps slipping back down the mountain.

My Friend pushes a rock up Yucca Mountain.

I'd like to make my position clear, as I do expect to be criticized for my views—that's fair. But clarity is in order. I adamantly oppose, I thoroughly oppose, I absolutely oppose the transportation of nuclear waste materials through Clark County Nevada.

Today I want to address what I consider to be a major disconnect in the nuclear waste policy debates. The public has shown great support for the political leaders who are making the Sisyphean struggle in opposing the placement of the waste dump at Yucca Mountain. The <u>Las Vegas Review Journal</u> has demonstrated this support in their polls over several years. The public has taken a very high profile ownership over desert lands 70 miles from Las Vegas. Yet among this public, only 10% were born in Nevada. Among this public, the average resident has been in southern Nevada only since 1990. The average resident came here three years or more after Congress designated Yucca Mountain as the only site to be considered for nuclear waste. Yet they take ownership pride in the desert lands 70 miles away!

I guess I am an old-timer. I came to Las Vegas in 1980. In each of my 22 years here I have found two or three occasions per year in which I have actually driven a car to Carson City or Reno. A car, on highways. Many times I have driven through or by Mercury, Indian Springs, Beatty, Goldfield, Tonopah, Coaldale and Hawthorne. I truly wonder if our new average Nevadans have even one time driven the same route. This is where I sense a disconnect. The outspoken opponents of Yucca Mountain are very vocal about dangers that lurk somewhere out in a distant space unfamiliar to them, while they are exceedingly silent on the many other kinds of waste products that are daily surrounding them on the streets where they do drive, and in the neighborhoods that they do see every day. They and our protesting politicians are quite silent about the waste encompassed by: our high student drop out rates, our nation leading statistics in drunk driving deaths, lung cancer cases, teen-age suicides, later year's suicides, teen pregnancies and the prevalence of compulsive gambling among our citizens. I have never heard their protests against smoking in our grocery stores. You are hearing mine right now.

Accompanying the public silence is an expected lack of adequate public funding for public education, community health and mental health programs, and public safety programs. Just a year ago the waste dump protestors voted against a children's hospital, libraries, and increased fire protection.

This Statue dedicated to 'The Teacher' is in Iquitos, Peru. It is not in Las Vegas.

While all people—not just Nevadans—tend to maximize risks that are quite remote and to minimize risks in their daily midst, we seem to go it one better than the rest. If the nuclear waste does not come through Clark County, the danger of the nuclear waste will not be in our midst. A danger that is at least eight years away (the waste facility will be operational after 2010) will not be a danger on our streets and in our neighborhoods. Yet over the same next eight years, we will tolerate without a whimper the social maladies that belie any notion that our new average population has taken any ownership whatsoever in the Las Vegas community. The real waste dump has been accumulating dangerous pollutants right here for quite some time. It is for the residents of southern Nevada to show they buy into the community in which they live, before their protests about some remote far away lands will resonate with the sound and energy necessary to push that rock over the mountain.

—January 22, 2002

Chapter 6. Le Reve: The Dream, Not a Memory

Le Reve—the dream—not a memory, but a dream—of the future. A gambler never looks back. Like a child learning to walk, he never dwells upon the last fall, but rather the next step, the next stake, the next wager.

Las Vegas is a gambler. Yesterday is gone, our world is tomorrow, the next show, the next attraction, the next resort, the next wager.

We keep running, always looking forward. That is our spirit, our sustenance, our life. Our dreams are not memories, they are of things to come, our dreams—Le Reve.

John F. Kennedy met the mob and his girlfriends at the Sands. Did we put up a plaque commemorating the history? No. We blew up the building. Tomorrow promised the Venetian. Howard Hughes bribed a presidential candidate so that Hughes could win the permission to purchase the Landmark. The bribe led to a break-in, and then to the resignation of President Nixon. Do we have a marker celebrating the origins of Watergate? We do not. Instead we blew up the Landmark. We made room for tomorrow with a parking lot for an expanded convention center. Jimmy Hoffa's teamsters loaned money for the construction of the Dunes. He fell from grace, but he wanted to return to power in his union. So he cooperated with federal prosecutors, and he told them about teamster loans to Las Vegas. He disappeared forever. Do we have a memorial for Hoffa on the Strip? No. We blew up the Dunes, we made way for tomorrow and the Bellagio.

We turn our backs on yesterdays, we gamble on tomorrows. If Las Vegas dwelled upon its unsavory past, on the losses of the past, we all might just as well fold up our tents and like the Bedouins of the desert, ride off into some murky sunset somewhere else. We don't. Instead, people move here. We build for the future. And our heros put their money on the future. Benjamin Siegel, Howard Hughes, Kirk Kerkorian, Sheldon Adelson, more recently George Maloof, and now, once again, Steve Wynn.

Landmark: Origins of Watergate.

After the M.G.M. bought the Mirage, Wynn could have folded up his tent, after the stock market tumbled, after 9-11 disrupted life in the nation and devastated the tourism industry, he could have folded up his tent. But like our other Las Vegas heros—our casino gamblers, and our casino developers—he chose to brush off, indeed to blow-up, the past and look only to his next wager.

Le Reve, his dream, will bring 1.8 billion dollars of capital investment to the Strip, along with 2500 new rooms, 18 new restaurants, lakes and a new golf course, an eight story high mountain, shops and a Ferrari and Maserati dealership. But Le Reve is not just must-see bricks and mortar, water and dirt. It is an endorsement that may lead to a new wave of development and to an expanded visitor base for Las Vegas. We must not only applaud Mr. Steve Wynn's next wager, his roll of the dice, but we should stand behind him and put our money on the pass line. Le Reve is our dream too.

—November 13, 2002

The Desert Inn in the 1950's. The resort is the site of Steve Wynn's new Le Reve. (Courtesy Special Collections, UNLV)

Chapter 7. Where's Aladdin's Genie?

Big projects are for big boys. The Aladdin is a big project, unfortunately it is woefully undercapitalized. Its owners are not "the big boys." The Aladdin is surrounded by big casinos owned by large resort corporations—the MGM-Mirage, Park Place, Mandalay Resorts. The Aladdin owners do not have extensive ownership experience in Las Vegas casinos. One major partner has casino experience in a very different market—London, England. There the casinos are not even allowed to advertise, and players must be members of a private club.

The Aladdin owners are not connected to other large American properties which can help them market their facility. These are problem areas that can be overcome—with money.

What the Aladdin organization has is a beautiful casino and shopping property that needs a lot of promotion as well as critical renovations—ergo a restructuring of entrance ways onto Las Vegas Boulevard. If the owners had deep pockets, they could spend the money and make a go of it, and that would be great for Las Vegas, because the Aladdin is a wonderful addition among the other new mega-resorts of the Strip.

Instead, we can only hope that one of the mega-resort corporations—Park Place, MGM-Mirage, Mandalay—or one of the lingering billionaires out there—a Branson, Ichon, or Gates—will step forth and buy a large share of the project.

I often comment on proposed legalizations of casino gambling. I tell residents of these "hopeful" jurisdictions that there is something worse than having casinos or not having casinos. What is worse? Having casinos, and having them go broke. A casino going down is bad all the way around. People who shifted careers and purchased homes and settled into a community with their new casino jobs have their lives miserably impacted. So do suppliers who have geared up their assembly lines and hired new staff to meet needs of the new customer. So do governments that come to rely upon the taxation income from the casinos, so do communities that rely on the spin-off economic benefits of resort casinos.

Aladdin's Genie: Real or Fading Away.
(Courtesy of Special Collections, UNLV)

It is ironic that the last major casino closed by governmental action in Nevada was the Aladdin in 1979. That closing so shocked the community that the state adopted a new policy for placing troubled properties into receivership, to be run by state-selected operators, as an alternative to closing their doors. We can hope that the Aladdin will not come to that end, but that a deep pockets partner will step forth soon.

It is especially gratifying that at this moment the premier casino operator of the last two decades, Steve Wynn, is back in the game on the Strip. His reappearance with a new mega casino proposal at the Desert Inn site gives Las Vegas a needed boost of optimism, and should encourage a prospective buyer for the Aladdin.

There is another irony. At this moment, the Nevada Gaming Commission is exploring policies regarding monopolies among our local casino ownership. While bigness can mean badness, we should not assume that it is. Baring the appearance of predatory practices among the "big boys" to destroy competitors through unfair competition, we should assume that the big ownership groups help

Las Vegas. It was a Howard Hughes that pulled us away from Mob casino domination. It was Kirk Kerkorian and the Hiltons that energized Las Vegas when corporate ownership was permitted after 1969. And the last round of building has been by giant concerns—the Bellagio, Venetian, Paris, and Mandalay Bay—three run by corporations and one by a billionaire. Big is good for Las Vegas. It is the big connected properties not small independent houses that attract the tourists who seek out the entertainment capital of the world from among other choices. We should not punish the big operators unless their actions demonstrate badness.

Las Vegas was built on successful casino operations. Let us hope that a big successful operator with deep pockets comes forth to rescue the Aladdin. It is a beautiful place, I sure hope we can keep it.

—September 10, 2001

Chapter 8. Las Vegas: Another Detroit?

Michael Moore's film "Roger and Me" won much acclaim including several 1989 "Best Documentary Film" awards. Moore focused upon General Motors factory closings in his hometown, Flint, Michigan.

Yet while thousands of auto workers in Flint and Detroit lost their jobs, the corporation was making profits as operations were moved to Mexico. Profits came even though General Motors lost market shares to Japanese car makers. The company's profits went to top executives and to shareholders who had little connection to Michigan.

The Michigan downsizing can be explained. There was groupthink as executives failed to see market demand for efficient cars. Then they found it easier to build factories in places with cheap labor. Foreign venues could easily compete with Michigan cars—they simply build cars people wanted to buy. Also the auto workers' union acquiesced in silence as Michigan factories closed. The union like management had grown old, and their concern was more for union executives than workers.

Detroit now has Casinos: Is Las Vegas also trying to be like Detroit?

23

Michigan was a one-industry venue. Michigan had a monopoly in car production. Then competitors came with new products and new plant locations. General Motors sold out a state that had nurtured the company since the first days of the Twentieth Century.

Sounds almost like Nevada. We had a monopoly in casinos. Then competitors came with new products and new plant locations. Might Las Vegas becomes another Detroit, another Flint?

I spoke at the state tourism conference in 1991. I concluded that "the factors that brought decay to Michigan are not major concerns for the Nevada casino industry." I said our owners and executives were locally-oriented. And Nevada companies were not building elsewhere, indeed, our state's "Foreign Gaming Law" imposed barriers on such investments. Through the 1990s, I held to this conclusion.

However, now America has experienced the 9-11 attacks. Our local casino industry reacted with a corporate attitude not often seen here before, an attitude we would expect from Roger Smith of General Motors. For the first time, our industry made massive layoffs. Groupthink hit the Strip, and the unions in Las Vegas reacted in silence. No, I take that back, they did protest, but only when a local entrepreneur bucked the negative groupthink of the Park Places and MGMs, and he opened the Palms only a month after the 9-11 disaster. The unions couldn't cope with people being given jobs—oh, and also the freedom to decide on their own if they wanted unions. The unions hadn't protested when their friends in management at the biggest casino companies announced plans to make their new capital investments in riverboats in Illinois, Indian casinos in California, or in new private casinos in Macau. The state had modified its foreign gaming rule and such investments are now permitted.

Las Vegas is recovering from the 9-11 attacks. But many loyal casino workers remain unemployed. And a few weeks ago, talk about "March Madness," several casinos gave large bonuses to top executives—some over a million dollars each. The outrageous bonuses appeared to be given for successful implementation of layoff policies. Oh, well, Roger Smith got a bonus of several millions of dollars when he retired from General Motors—a lesson now heard, and endorsed, in Las Vegas.

George Maloof talking to a college class before he opens the Palms. He *Hired* workers after the tragedy of 9-11.

Will Las Vegas become another Flint, another Detroit? In 1991, I said "No." Today my answer would be much more tentative. We have taken some first big steps in that direction.

Soon Michael Moore may bring cameras to Las Vegas and make a sequel of "Roger and Me." Maybe he will call it something like "Berry and the Pirates," or maybe "Gary and Me."

—April 23, 2001

Chapter 9. A Labor Peace: A Win-Win Game

Most of the time Las Vegas is a city of winners and losers. The casinos are most often the winners in a zero-sum game called gambling. But guess what, we just saw the results of a positive-sum game in Las Vegas. The successful negotiations of culinary union contracts truly represent a win win game. The casinos are winners, no surprise, but the other players are winners also—the workers are winners and so too are the residents of Las Vegas.

First of all, the workers achieved all of their bargaining goals, they received an appropriate raise in wages, some important improvements in work rules, and most importantly, they kept health care coverage for their families. The union won their victory because they had the facts on their side, and also because they stayed focused during negotiations. While there was some silliness away from the table, a cafeteria scuffle, leaflets sent to out-of-town tour directors, the diversions were few. The union rallied the workers in a show of strength, and the union stayed on message for its victory.

But the casinos also were victorious. For one thing, they atoned, at least a little bit, for their quick layoff policies after September 11. But most importantly, by agreeing to pay the increasing costs of family health care for workers, they headed off a political battle they don't want. Culinary workers are not highly paid. If the casinos did not pick up health care costs, many workers would turn to public assistance to pay for medical services. If that would happen, lawmakers would be almost compelled to support a major tax increase on the gambling industry. Now that won't happen. Also, the casinos just purchased five years of labor peace. With good relations with their workers, the large casinos can now plan for the next wave of major expansions in Las Vegas.

The public also is a big winner. The general taxpayer will not have to underwrite the health costs of workers. More importantly, the settlement helps the Las Vegas economy prosper, which, in turn, benefits all. Really, the negotiations came down to a question of who gets the money. The casinos are doing well and their gaming wins are rising. The money can go to casino executives in big bonuses, it can go to bottomline profits, or it can go to the workers. The workers will spend the lion's share of their compensation package inside the Las Vegas economy. The money will be recycled and it will help all local businesses. But many casino executives do not live in Las Vegas, and in any case few can be expected to spend their bonuses in Las Vegas. Profits can be good as they promote reinvestments in Las Vegas growth. However, as the major casino properties are now tied to national companies, they are directing reinvestment moneys to other locations—MGM Mirage is spending over a billion dollars on a new Atlantic City casino.

GAMBLING ECONOMICS IN A BATHTUB

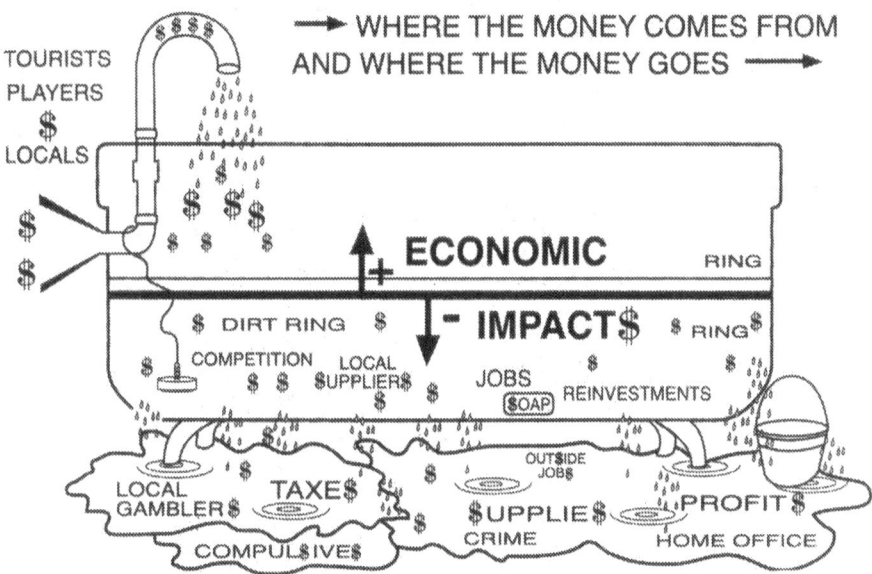

Gambling Economics in a Bathtub: Higher Wages keeps More Money in the Las Vegas Economy.

The real bottomline is simple to understand. All Las Vegans win when casino workers get a bigger share of the money. The negotiations are over and indeed we are all winners—and that's a new kind of game for Las Vegas.

—May 29, 2002

Chapter 10. Just Do It! Oscar

(This following commentary was broadcast following the Mayor's State 2002 State of the City address).

Oscar Goodman is the flamboyant mayor of Las Vegas. Some might even call him "loveable." He received considerable renown in earlier days as the legal counsel for persons considered to be (alleged to be) attached to organized crime establishments. As Mayor he champions the City and the downtown casino area which has suffered decline over recent decades. He envisions many different schemes to reverse the fortunes of this aging area of the City. These include schemes for making money that could be used to help the City. Some might think that he seeks to make a silk purse out of a sow's ear.

As a professor of public administration I seek to interpret struggles of leaders today by using models of behaviors from past times.

When I think of Mayor Oscar Goodman and the struggles he has set on his own plate in his State of the City address, I tend to think of Don Quixote, Hercules, and also to my favorite character from ancient mythology—a man named Sisyphus.

Sisyphus had tricked the gods, and so when he at last descended into the depths of hell, he was given a rather arduous task. He was told that he had to push a rock up a hill and over the top. However, each time he neared the peak of the hill, the rock slipped out of his hands, and it rolled back to the bottom. His task was undone, so he had to go back to the bottom, and start pushing again.

So it has been for Sisyphus during his eternity in hell. So too it seems it is for Mayor Oscar Goodman's dreams of big league sports teams, a new academic medical center downtown, and an end to the local homeless problem. These are indeed Sisyphean sized enigmas, great big rocks that will never get pushed over a mountain. Or are they?

Big league teams don't appreciate the marketing possibilities in American's fastest growing city. Many of the homeless love the street life here, and the cost of a medical center is prohibitive. Rocks too big, mountains too steep.

But what could Sisyphus have done with the rock and the mountain if he had not willingly accepted his fate? Maybe he could have dug in and put some cleats on his shoes. Maybe he could have used some pulleys and levers. Maybe he could have dug a pit so the back sliding rocks would not have gone all the way to the bottom. Maybe he could have used the faith of a mustard seek and just moved the mountain, or he could have used a blasting cap and blown off the top of the mountain. Maybe he could have burrowed a tunnel through the mountain.

How about it Oscar? I think you have a blasting cap, I think you have a tool for digging that tunnel.

**Oscar Goodman and his client the notorius (and late) Tony Spilatro.
(Courtesy of Special Collections, UNLV)**

You have it in your hands, don't let others deter you. Take your idea of a Las Vegas internet gambling site, and sell it to a jurisdiction where internet gambling is legal today. Don't be set back by those worried about the City's reputation—those people are not going downtown to Fremont Street today, they are not going to the minor league baseball games there, and they do not go to local hospitals to receive specialized medical care.

Internet gambling is legal in almost every country in the world today. The Las Vegas site could be run from Canada or maybe even Mexico. The Las Vegas brand name is worth a lot of money. A Las Vegas internet site would be an honest site that would attract gamers from everywhere internet gaming is legal. Do it. Now.

Dedicate the City's profits from the venture to a downtown medical research center. The revenues could pay for such a center in five years. Do it. Use some of the money to enhance and reconfigure the Jean, Nevada, internment facility, to be a care facility for the homeless—a place where they can receive much better services and support than they can receive on our sidewalks and at the backdoors of the downtown casinos. Use the money to promote more healthy diversified growth in Las Vegas and the major leaguers will come.

Mr. Mayor you have a Sisyphean task, but you can blast a hole right through the mountain. You have the tools. Do it! Now!

—January 11, 2002

Chapter 11. Common Cause, Uncommon Valor?

The political action group Common Cause has set its sites on the casino gambling industry. We had better be prepared to be the target of some good marksmen. It is time to search for armor.

Quite frankly, I wish that Common Cause would take aim at the nation's high schools for pushing junk food and sugared drinks in their cafeterias, or perhaps the auto companies for enticing our purchases of gas-guzzling dangerous SUVs, but they haven't. The fact that our society has greater problems, more important problems than compulsive gambling offers us little defense. Compulsive gambling is a problem.

We must also be aware that Common Cause is led by Scott Harshbarger—you are going to be hearing that name a lot—Scott Harshbarger. Scott is the former attorney general of Massachusetts. As such he began the class action suits against the tobacco industry. Our attorney general Frankie Sue del Pappa was his partner in that effort. She won. He won. Billions of dollars. Scott Harshbarger knows what he is doing.

Our casino industry has done very little to head-off what could be a highly contentious and extremely expensive set of law suits. Even if the verdicts ultimately go in favor of the casinos, the industry could be severely damaged in the process. Our nightly news screens will be bringing the nation the emotional images of people who have suffered greatly because of compulsive gambling. A spokesman for MGM Mirage said these people represent less than 3% of the American adults—well that means there are as many as six million tear-jerking stories that might be told. I've heard some of them, they can be quite grabbing.

One of the leading casino companies, Harrahs, recently announced a nationwide advertising campaign to encourage its patrons to gamble "prudently." That's not bad. The CEO of Harrahs said "there are a lot of times you shouldn't gamble." Like when you are underage, drunk, or depressed. Good words. But we need action not just words if we are going to convey the notion to the public that we do not welcome compulsive gamblers into our casinos. There is no doubt that the Harrahs ads will help the company's image. Where the ads were test marketed, the brand name recognition of Harrahs increased from 28% to 40%, but I hope that was not the goal of the ads. We need action not brand name recognition and appeals for more customers. We need to throw the compulsive gamblers out.

Do Casinos Push Drugs: Detroit's Motor City Casino is Pushing One.

If we do not do so, Mr. Scott Harshbarger and a set of smooth trial lawyers will make us wish we had. The law suits will cost our industry a lot more money than we may lose by getting rid of the action from troubled gamblers.

I was very bothered when I recently was invited to analyze some slot club records for a court case. The records had been successfully subpoenaed from a casino. If a local attorney can get the records through a court order, believe me, the records will be available when Mr. Harshbarger steps off the bench and up to the bar. I saw a play-by-play historical record of every play a gambler made at the slot machines of a casino. I saw the number of coins and the denomination of the coins put into each machine, I saw the exact number of minutes played on each machine, I saw the time of day, and I saw the record of coins out, and also points awarded from the slot clubs. What I saw was not absolute proof of compulsive gambling, but rather strong evidence that might make a jury think a player had a severe problem with gambling. I saw chasing behavior—that is increasing play and faster play after a string of losses. I saw evidence of binge behavior, play at machines that lasted through the night and well into the next day, 8-10-15 hours of consecutive play. Usually such binges started with a jackpot win in the first hour of play. I saw a record of play where the last machine played only took in one or two dollars—a record of playing until the last coin was gone.

The slot club records were not from Harrahs. But Harrahs wants to do something about compulsive gambling—hopefully something beyond increasing their name recognition 40%. Harrahs does have the largest slot club in America—-with millions of members. Guess what: Harrahs knows who the compulsive gamblers are. They have the records. They have the evidence, and Scott Harshbarger knows they have the evidence. It is time they look at their own computer records and say not what offer can we make to get these folks back, but how can we get these people to examine their behaviors—behaviors that could be very harmful. Harrahs and the other casinos must seriously consider writing to people with troubling records and suggesting they discuss the possibilities of them having major problems, and the casinos must be prepared to say if the evidence is sufficient, just as a bar must say to a known alcoholic, "You are no longer welcome, and we will ask you to leave if you come to our casino."

It is time for the casinos to "just say NO" to the compulsive gamblers. Let us do it before the law suits begin.

—June 13, 2002

Chapter 12. Nevada: The Promise or the Solution

The state of Nevada has finally spent some money on compulsive gambling. Unfortunately, the state did not spend the $196,000 doing anything about compulsive gambling. Instead, they spent it on a study to determine how many compulsive gamblers there are in the state. They didn't get much for their money. The answers were imprecise—between 2.1% and 6.4% of the population.

Actually, there have been over 100 such studies around the country, and those studies, including a national study, seem to encompass the range of results found for Nevada. Ergo, we learned nothing new. The national study found that about one per cent were compulsive gamblers, but the percentage doubled in locations where casino gambling was convenient. So the low range of 2.1% seems on target.

Sounds like a low number. Unfortunately, it means there are 30,000 resident compulsive gamblers in Nevada. (The adult population is approximately 1.5 million).

So what? Unless we can show that this number of compulsive gamblers is damaging to society, we need not spend more money on the issue. However, if real public costs are attached to compulsive gambling, that is another matter. But if there are costs, how high are the costs?

I participated in studies of Gamblers Anonymous members in other states. We asked the members about their gambling behaviors before they sought treatment, and about how they got money for gambling. We found that their behaviors resulted in the imposition of costs upon others outside of their families. In Wisconsin, a median state in our studies, the social costs of gambling amounted to $9400 per compulsive gambler per year. We found that the average compulsive gambler stole goods (or cash) worth $1733 per year. Lost productivity cost others $2726 per year, and unemployment compensation cost $213. Criminal procedures, from arrests, to courts, prison and probation cost $1765, and other court matters cost $847 per compulsive gambler per year. Welfare costs were $336, and therapy costs paid by the public amounted to $361.

**The Harbor Center for Treating Compulsive Gamblers: It's Not in Las Vegas –
It's in Baltimore.**

However, there were other costs which could not have dollar signs attached. A high divorce rate was caused by gambling problems, with domestic failures burdening children with both neglect and abuse. Nearly one-fourth of the compulsive gamblers attempted suicide. And many had physical afflictions not factored into the costs.

If Nevada is but a median state, then, we can expect that 30,000 adult compulsive gamblers will impose costs of $284 million dollars a year on all Nevadans, including those who don't gamble, and those who gamble responsibly.

Carson City, we have a problem. The problem does not need more study, it needs action. Action means education in our schools and in our public media, it means warning signs, it means intervention and even exclusion from gambling facilities, it means stopping credit for compulsive gamblers, and taking them out of promotions schemes such as offered by slot clubs (where the known evidence in casino records will tell the casino just who the problem gamblers are), it means funding hotlines and treatment programs.

If we can just cut the Nevada numbers down to the national averages, it will be worth well over a hundred million dollars to our citizens. It is worth an appropriation a bit more that the $196,000 we spent this past year.

—April 19, 2002

Chapter 13. A Lottery for Nevada

As a student of gambling, I often make comparisons among different kinds of games and gaming venues. Generally I support the tourist destination resort casinos. We offer these in abundance in Nevada. Generally I condemn government lotteries. We do not have a government-authorized lottery in Nevada.

I oppose lotteries for several reasons. First, I don't think governments should be in the gambling business. Gambling enterprise should be conducted by private concerns that can be regulated and severely disciplined if they ever violate critical canons of integrity. I especially object to governments advertising their gambling operations with an implicit plea that citizens have some sort of civic duty to engage in the gambling activity—to support education or some other "good cause."

Second, I do not like the idea of having gambling shoved into the faces of citizens whether they want to gamble or not. We in Nevada have gambling shoved in our faces each time we go into our grocery stores—with the presence of slot machines. But the lotteries are even worse. Lottery outlets are ubiquitous and pervasive. Lottery advertising surrounds the citizenry. Whether we like gambling or not, we should recognize that where it is legal, citizens should have the right to engage in the activity and also the right to avoid contact with the activity. Moreover, children should not be constantly exposed to the activity.

Third, one of the worse features of the lotteries is that they are rotten games. Typically a lottery ticket that costs one dollar will return fifty cents to players in prize money, expend ten to fifteen cents in expenses, and leave 35 to 40 cents for government causes. On the other hand, even the worse games in Nevada casinos return ninety cents of each dollar played to the players.

Should Nevada have a lottery? The answer would seem rather obvious. But maybe it isn't. Surprise. My answer is "yes." We should have a lottery in Nevada.

A Powerball Ticket

A recent poll found that two-thirds of Nevadans want a lottery. We should recognize their wishes. Moreover, thousands of Nevadans drive to the California each week to buy lotto tickets which offer the dream chance to win multi-million dollar prizes—prizes much larger than promised by our mega-bucks games. There is a demand for this kind of lottery among Nevadans.

I support a state lottery for Nevada, but I strongly dissent from establishing a lottery on the model followed by 38 other states and the District of Columbia. Our lottery should not seek to offer games that are very much like games already offered in our casinos. Our citizens already have easy access to games like the instant lotteries—after all slots are just like instant lotteries. Some states actually call slot machines "video lottery terminals." We don't need lottery numbers games. Our casinos offer keno and bingo games which duplicate features of these lottery games. What casinos don't offer is progressive lotto games. Those are the lottery games we should have.

Moreover it is imperative that the lottery games Nevada has will offer players (ergo, the gambling public) a return of 85 to 90 cents on the dollar played—or more.

My plan is very simple and direct. The Nevada Gaming Commission should approve the sale of Lotto America Powerball tickets in casinos. The casino would hold a sales commission of seven percent basically equalling the return they take on average casino games. They would pay the normal gaming tax on this revenue. The players would receive about 50 cents in prize money, and the government would receive 35 to 40 cents on each ticket sold. However, if the government returns its share of the money to programs to help players, then the players' return would not be 50 cents, but a respectable 85 to 90 cents. I propose that the state's profits from the sale of Powerball tickets be dedicated to mental health programs in the state, and that these programs include a comprehensive program for education, prevention, and treatment for compulsive gambling. The casinos would limit all exterior advertising of Powerball.

With such a lottery program, ticket sales would not directly compete with casino games. Additionally, like casino games, the sale of these tickets in casinos could result in gaming activity by many non-residents. Californians who cannot play this specific lotto game (their state lotto game is different) may come to Nevada when the Powerball prize is exceptionally large. Also tourists from many other locations might be attracted to the games. Many Nevadans who are now going to California to play lotto games would shift much of their patronage back to Nevada casinos.

The powerball sales would yield an estimated amount of money probably in excess of $40 million a year for programs to help troubled people in the state, many of whom would be problem gamblers in need of mental health services. This money would serve the state well. The state legislature has refused to appropriate any money at all for problem gambling programs, compared with a dozen or more other states which see it as an obligation due to the fact that they receive public funds from gambling activity. Nevada's refusal to deal with these problems at some level opens our basic industry to unneeded attacks from anti-gambling interests.

The author holds a Cuban lottery ticket.

In the recent legislative session there was an abortive attempt to initiate a lottery. Legislators and others believed in the necessity to change the state constitution in order to have a lottery. If the state were to set up a state-run lottery with many games and with a new state agency, it is likely that the state constitution might have to be amended. The 1864 constitution prohibits lotteries. However, the Nevada Gaming Commission is empowered to allow casinos to offer gambling games. The precedence has been clearly set that casinos under direction of the Commission can allow lottery games—for instance bingo is a lottery game, so is keno, so are all wheel games, and so are many of the games played on machines. The super-prize on-line computerized progressive lotto games such as the Powerball game did not exist in 1864. The constitution writers in Nevada were addressing paper-ticket sale lottery games popular at the time outside of casinos. The Nevada Gaming Commission clearly could allow casinos to sell Powerball tickets. It could be done immediately. It would be meet the desires and demands of the citizens. It would be good for the state.

—August 29, 2001

Chapter 14. Fat Dog Don't Run No Rabbit, Hungry Dog Do.

The Nevada political scene winds down as another legislative session is ending with budgets slashed and funds for needed programs for an expanding population disappearing.

Those of us in institutions relying on state funding seem more concerned than the general population, but then it is the general population that is being sold short by the policy makers.

This professor has no complaints about his own salary at the University, after all I have many years-in-grade and I am doing about as well as a person of my rank would do elsewhere. I am not looking elsewhere, but many of my talented younger colleagues are, and we need their skills here. But the budget does not just leave salaries without much growth, it attacks programs that help serve growing numbers of high school graduates with training for positions which will allow them to remain in Nevada to answer the needs of the expanding public, whether in education as teachers, in hospitals as nurses or administrators, in government as public safety officers, and social service providers, or in the private and public sector as engineers, accountants, economists and in myriad other professions and specialties.

The irony is that we are the fastest growing state in the Union, and our state economy is growing, and all about us we see wealth. We see it in the new gated-communities that are even invading the territory of North Las Vegas—soon to be our newest Green Valley. We see it in road development, new water systems, in airport construction, in the bustle of traffic on our streets and highways. We see it in continued growth in the gaming industry. Yet somehow, the policy makers of our state cry "poverty." There is a disconnect.

We need more tax revenue. But we need to look at ourselves as the source of new tax revenues. As a state we have given well over a half a century to the notion that others—ala tourists via casino taxes—should pay our tax bills for us. This has nurtured an attitude among us that others should pay for our burdens, that others should pay for the services we need and we demand—and I don't just mean salaries for public employees. We need new taxes that will hit us all, and hit us all hard enough to know that we should care about our government services, and how they are being delivered—whether they are being delivered with efficiency, with results, and yes, by people of integrity. Unfortunately, with low taxes, we tend not to care that much about whether our services are shoddy and our leaders ineffective. Witness our very low voter turnouts. While I have been a Nevada Native for over twenty years I still remember my property taxes elsewhere. Certainly the average Nevadan—one who came here since 1990—is fully aware that our property taxes are very very low. That average Nevadan should also realize that the costs of services placed upon the government by new home development are not covered by the tax levies on property. My lawn service charges almost equal the taxes I pay for schools, libraries, and public safety. Pool cleaning services often are more than property tax levies. Most condo fees and fees for living in "gated communities" greatly exceed property taxes. Ergo, the property tax is the place where my vote goes for new higher taxes. For governments these are stable and reliable taxes. It is important that these taxes are paid by all our citizens—and mainly by our citizens. Home owners pay the taxes. Renters pay the taxes. And even Senator Joe Neal can be happy if we raise property taxes, for the largest individual property holders are the casinos—they too will share in the increased tax burden. But they will "share," they will not be expected to carry all my community burdens for me.

It is true that our low tax mentality has been good for our economic growth. Nevada is favored by seniors precisely because we do not have an income tax. The one tax change that would encourage me to leave the state upon retirement would indeed be a state income tax.

Our sales taxes have been skewed to fall heavily upon non-residents. We don't need to add anything here, although we could probably trade a lower rate for getting rid of all of the special interest exemptions from the sales tax. Moreover, we shouldn't nickel and dime the citizenry with a myriad of nuisance taxes that perpetuate the myth that we can get government services for nothing. For the same reason we should avoid new gimmicks such as tapping the Estate Tax Fund or creating a general lottery to help any special cause.

We need the better services across the board and we better start stepping forth and saying, "Yes, we can carry our own burdens, we can pay our own way." The leaders of the state of Nevada have treated the citizenry of Nevada as if we were fat dogs that could not take care of our selves without the help of outsiders. Well, fat dog don't run no rabbit. Hungry dog do. It is time we grow up and become adults in our role as citizens. It is time we push ourselves away from a food table set by others. It is time we run the rabbit and get our own food. It is time we start taking care of ourselves.

—May 15, 2001

Alf: A Hungry Dog
(Courtesy of Mary Riddel)

Chapter 15. Abolish the Legislature

On January first 1883, Nevada state attorney general M.A. Murphy recommended to Governor John Kinkaid that the legislature meet only once every four years. He suggested that this would save the state a lot of money. I am sure that it would. I guess the figure is 80,000 dollars a day.

The truth seems to be that the legislature could meet every hour, or once a day, everyday, or once a week, once a year, or once a decade, and it really wouldn't matter all that much. The Nevada legislature appears to be rather irrelevant. They are the Nancy Reagan legislature—they are best at just saying "No."

They might be quite adept at representing well a people who loves to just say "No"—to libraries, children hospitals, fire and police services. Yet it seems quite a waste that they have to gather together and utilize the energy flowing from the capital's air-conditioners and light-bulbs. It was especially absurd that they met for a special session to draw their district lines. Like does it matter if our legislator lives on the east or west side of Pecos, or on the north or southside of Wigwam? It simply doesn't matter who gets elected. It isn't funny, but it is tragic that one house was Republican, one house Democrat, and even with a governor to furnish suggestions, we did not have one genuine idea coming forth from anywhere about how to deal with public policy problems in the state.

I suggest we go one better than attorney general M. A. Murphy, and cease having the legislature meet at all. Instead, we could simply have a three person panel get together and set forth state policy. The panel would consist of Bill Bible, the leader of the Nevada Resorts Association, Frank Fahrenkopf, the director of the American Gaming Association, and a third voice representing R+R advertising. Unless they speak together the legislature isn't going to do anything anyway, and the legislature is willing to step up on any issue if they unanimously push the lawmakers.

There is a serious agenda that only this panel of three can deal with. I think they would see the sense in doing the following.

They would see the sense in raising the casino tax to 8%, and collaterally eliminating local and state fees on each machine or table according to some formula that could be understood only by an anthropologist who deals with hieroglyphics. While the tax increase would only be minimal under these conditions, it would be important. It would bring Nevada's tax level up to the basic state levies in South Dakota, Mississippi, and New Jersey, the latter two being the second and third largest casino states in the union. No longer would casino spokesmen have to answer the embarrassing question: "why are you willing to pay higher taxes elsewhere?" The tax level should apply to all casinos—even the small ones are owned by millionaires—and to machines in bars and grocery stores. These should be linked together in computerized reporting systems.

The three could also raise industry funds for a study of the fairness of casinos taxes. Here I would like them to explore whether other taxpayers are subsidizing casinos allowing them to hire lowly-paid employees who move to the state with large families demanding services not paid for through taxes the employees pay. Now it might be that the 8% will cover the extra load this places upon the school district and other service providers, but then, maybe the study would show the casinos should pay more, and if so, the panel could raise the tax level above 8%.

Abolish the Legislature
(Courtesy of Andrew Harvey, Nevada State Museum)

The panel should be very willing to see money spent at significant levels for compulsive gambling problems. Maybe the money could come from having the state join Lotto America for its Powerball game. Lottery games are a bad bet, and most Nevadans would avoid instant ticket games—slots give much better paybacks than numbers games; keno is a better game. But they would like to play lotto games with prizes into the hundreds of millions of dollars, because our casinos don't offer those games. A stand alone state lottery game wouldn't get a jackpot any higher than megabucks, so it might be worth a try to join a multi-state game. The proceeds from the state's share of the Powerball game could be designated entirely for substance abuse education, mitigation and treatment. This would include compulsive gambling problems.

Forty to fifty million dollars a year would make a difference. It is pitiful that one state senator proposed to spend $250,000 in this area. The bill was unanimously supported by the legislators, but somehow this senator, who is purported to be one of the best according to the Review Journal, couldn't get the bill passed. Maybe that's what makes a senator effective in Nevada, proposing bills that fail without anyone having to oppose them.

Now some may argue that I am suggesting that we scrap democratic government in Nevada. Sounds like it, I guess, but then America was formed on the principle of no taxation without representation, and just maybe there is a reverse to that—a principle that says no representation without taxation. Since the only taxes the legislature wants to levy are on non-resident tourists, I'm not sure that residents need the legislature in order to maintain American constitutional principles.

No, I relish the thought that a panel from the gambling, that is gaming industry, could more effectively govern us directly, than they can in the indirect feeble way they are doing so at the moment.

—June 19, 2001

Chapter 16. Carson City, We Have a Crisi$

We have a crisis in America, we have a crisis in Nevada. It is a crisis of safety, of terrorism, of war; it is a crisis of resolve.

We may have an economic crisis, we may not have an economic crisis. This we do not know. Our political leaders and our business leaders admit as much; they do not know how long our national commerce will be affected by difficulties in transportation.

Yet while they admit they don't know how long economic problems will continue—a day a week, a month, or more—the casino industry leaders have reacted as if a major depression is imminent. The mass layoffs in the casino industry were knee jerk reactions, not reasoned responses to our crisis.

The governor's compassion for the fired employees is nice, but he now wants all of us to step forth and help the former workers—banks should give them loans, utility bills should be deferred, mortgage companies should defer housing payments, even the university should not ask for tuition payments. Every one is asked to help the newly unemployed—everyone except, that is, the casino industry. Why doesn't the governor simply ask the industry to hire the workers back until the future economic situation is clarified?

Moreover while the governor joins the industry in lamenting the weakened economy, he fails to show any resolve in correcting what is known. We will have a shortfall in the state budget this year. But not just this year. We have a long-term fiscal crisis in our state because our tax structure is flawed. The governor now has an opportunity to call the legislature into special session and ask the lawmakers to consider new revenue sources for the state. We cannot deal with our fiscal shortfalls simply by "tightening our belts". We've already been there. We are thin. Yet thousands of newcomers move to our state each month, and they, as well as all the rest of us need services; we need new funding arrangements.

I have talked about this before. In 1981 we shifted the tax base from the very reliable stable property tax, to the unreliable sales tax. We had solid surpluses before, we have been on the edge of deficits ever since. We must take another look at our very very low property tax rates. We could also remove several, indeed all, exemptions from the sales tax—or at least all but the food exemption. I have mentioned that the sale of powerball tickets in casinos could bring us an additional $40 million or more for mental health services that are woefully lacking. After we have done our part as citizens, we can then look to the casinos. They should then be willing to do their part. I recommend that they agree to an 8% gross win tax in return for removal of state and local fees on individual games. This would represent an effective one per cent increase in their rate of taxation. The 8% tax would put them on par with New Jersey casinos, and it would remove questions about why they are willing to pay more elsewhere than here.

We can make some budget cuts, perhaps defer construction projects, defer some absurd projects like Henderson State University, reassess the elementary class size reductions—after all, the greatest at-risk students, the ones dropping out are in middle school and high school, defer some public wage increases (like mine for instance), but still we will need new revenues.

The Governor's Mansion in Carson City: We Have a Crise$.
(Courtesy of Special Collections, UNLV)

The governor is a leader, he has been a leader throughout his private and public career. This business-as-usual tighten-your-belt attitude is not becoming him. He needs to show some resolve. I think we are ready to follow. Our leader needs to show some leadership.

—October 2, 2001

Chapter 17. Maybe We Should Try "Tax and Spend"

Two powerful forces in politics are incrementalism and the status quo. Policy makers find change fraught with danger, so when pushed toward decisions they seek the smallest change possible.

Governor Kenny Guinn has an opportunity to challenge these forces. He has appointed a panel to make a comprehensive review of state taxes.

Past politicians occasionally risked changes, but past changes are now the status quo. The status quo and incrementalism put us where we are—in a state fiscal crisis. We need major changes to end the crisis.

The Department of Public Administration at UNLV recently hosted five governors for a discussion. The audience left with a sense of pride that our small state produced these leaders. They are men of integrity who rose above party to deliver policies for the good of all Nevadans, policies supported by rational thought at the time. Yet the decisions are now part of a status quo that needs to be fixed, especially in the area of decisions to tax and spend.

One governor championed civil rights, and in order to get legislation passed for open housing, he needed one legislator's vote. He exchanged support for a new state college for the vote. He seized the political moment. The state was radiant with a new sense of justice, but then, the state also now has an inefficient institution that is a drain on the budget.

Another governor fought off a California-type proposal for slashing taxes and spending. He did so with a reasoned plan for shifting tax burdens from property taxes to sales taxes, a good move considering the alternative. Now the status quo finds the unreliable fickle retail sales tax hurting our state's ability to plan for needed services.

One governor embraced a worthy plan for class size reduction in primary grades. Now this idea is costing the state $100 million a year, and it is not producing results. Yet students most at-risk are in high schools where a high drop out rate is a national shame. There classes have 30 to forty-plus students. Status quo priorities are out of balance.

The last governor to raise gaming taxes did so with courage, but then promised gamers no more increases. Now it is a new decade, and a new century, and the status quo rates are not sufficient for our needs.

Governor Guinn has moved with caution. But one kind of caution that will be most harmful will be the maintenance of the status quo or some weak effort for more revenue through incremental means.

Where can his panel go? Casino taxes. Casinos are rich, right. Should they pay more for that reason? NO. They should pay the costs of services—all services—they receive, and the panel should consider if the non-casino taxpayers are subsidizing casinos by allowing them to offer lower wages to some workers. If their workers cannot, in turn, pay taxes that will cover costs of education and other services their families receive, then other taxpayers are paying the casinos' bills. This goes for other businesses too, especially building trades—where incidently there is no general business tax similar to the gaming tax. The panel should consider raising the worker head tax, and also real estate transfer fees.

The panel should also look at the very low property taxes we pay and ask if perhaps some residents are getting a free ride on many of the services they receive.

The governor's panel should consider forms of taxing wages. Perhaps they could look at piggy-back income taxes that would not require the creation of a state I.R.S., something we don't want. The panel should also ask how many services are received by the millions of visitors to our state.

They pay room taxes, sales taxes, gasoline taxes. It is legitimate to place burdens on them, they do receive services, but the effect of taxing outsiders has undesirable consequences. Over the years, Nevadans have developed the notion that unless someone else pays the bill, we would just as soon do without the services. This no-tax no-service philosophy did us well for a time, but it is now a part of a status quo that is hurting us. We also have to look at reckless spending—the class reduction boondoggle, and stupid ideas like creating more colleges to appease individual legislators.

Governor Guinn sat proudly on a platform shared by other governors who took risks, rejected the status quo, and made major decisions for the good of the entire state. It is not a bad tradition. I hope it is one Governor Guinn follows with new tax-and-spend policies.

December 11, 2001

Chapter 18. Meaningless Elections, Meaningless Democracy?

The French philosopher Rousseau stated that there never has been a real democracy, and there never will be.

Perhaps that should give comfort to the citizens of Nevada, but I don't think so. Governments can be more democratic or less democratic, and we are not doing a good job of moving toward the top of the list. Case in point—this year's elections and the most critical issue facing our state—taxation. Working definitions of democracy include notions such as "the people will know when things are bad," or "when the shoe pinches, they will respond at the ballot box." Good luck. We are facing a financial crises. We know the next state budget will be $250 million short if we are to just maintain our current level of services—levels that put us among the worse states on most items. We have to increase taxes.

The shoe is pinching. But where's the opportunity to go to the ballot box and say "let's change shoes, let's change leadership?" The opportunity is almost non-existent, the notion of democracy is illusive at best. Illusive? Perhaps one could say non-existent.

Start at the top, we are experiencing the fifth consecutive governor's election in which there is no contest. There is only one candidate. How can we say the shoe pinches?

Look at the legislative races. Look at the judicial races. No issues are expressed. There are only signs imposing visual pollution to go along with the sand and motor waste pollution we experience driving across our valley each day. The signs do nothing more that state the candidates' names. Issues—what about taxation? What about a discussion by each candidate regarding what each will do if elected. Will the governor, and the legislative candidates tell us if they endorse a business income tax, a personal income tax, a lottery, higher property taxes, a removal of exemptions from sales taxes, sales taxes on services, gaming taxes? And how much will each tax be? And for the judicial candidates, could they each please tell us if they will be cooperative in approving new taxes, or will they be inclined to render any efforts to increase taxes void for some reason or another?

Jimmy Carter Come Home: We Need You Here

If we are to have any semblance of intelligent democratic life in Nevada, we need answers from each candidate, BEFORE the elections.

This is what we need, but what did the governor and the legislators do during their last biennial love-fest? They appointed a commission of non-elected citizens to meet and come up with answers. And they made it very clear the commission should not give its recommended answers until AFTER the November 2002 elections. This is a travesty of justice and responsibility. This is a travesty of democracy.

Those who wish to be our leaders must speak out now. As citizens we cannot allow candidates to hide behind non-elected advisory boards until after the election.

It has to start with the governor. Mr. Guinn give us your tax plan NOW. Legislators, tell us your ideas to meet our crisis and tell us NOW. Judicial candidates, I am quite frankly unconcerned about your "integrity" "your Martindale Hubble rating" your "law degree" and whether you "care" about me, I want to know what you intend to do when you get power over taxation policies.

Politicians, I am sick of your aesthetically filthy polluting signs with their vacuous content. If you tell me what you will do about taxes when you are elected, at least I can take go to the polls and vote, and feel that my vote is more than just a futile exercise in waving the flag.

—August 8, 2002

Chapter 19. Golden Rules and Taxes

Golden Rule Number One: Do unto others, as you would have others do unto you.

Golden Rule Number Two: He who has the gold, makes the rules.

Nevada does have a fiscal crises. Nonetheless, in our recent election—or should I say non-election, Nevada politicians consciously chose NOT to discuss state finances. Accordingly they would be quite in error to suggest that as a result of winning their non-contests, they have a mandate to do anything about state taxes and spending. State leaders have legal authority to make decisions, but they do not have moral authority on these issues. In a democracy the public delegates policy making authority to leaders, but only to leaders who are forthright in presenting relevant views about policy options. Taxation with representation means representation based upon informed consent. No such consent has been rendered on Nevada fiscal issues.

But then perhaps this is the way it should be. A fiscal problem we do have, but the solutions should not be placed in the hands of our state leaders, because our Nevada problem is simply NOT a Nevada problem. It is a national problem.

Our state problem is not at all unique. Forty-five states have seen their public revenues fall in the last fiscal year. American state tax receipts are $40 billion behind where they were a year ago. A Nevada shortfall of $300 million is only typical.

Every state has been hurt because of the 9-11 attacks. Each has been hurt by the soft economy, by the stock market decline, and by federal budget cuts, especially cuts to programs the federal government mandates the states to finance. Medicaid is the worse villain.

Governor Guinn and legislators Perkins, Raggio, Shaffer, and Titus cannot solve these problems. Other states have tried to do so, and they only end up making irrational cuts in needed programs, or they add new revenue measures without thinking through consequences. Several states are seeking higher cigarette taxes, others are increasing college tuition, several are seeking expansion of gaming with slot machines in bars and at racetracks. We are pinning hopes on an unproven untried and inequitable gross receipts tax. Quick fixes, bad policy. The answers lie in Washington D.C. in the hands of Senators Reid and Ensign, Congresspersons Porter, Berkley, and Gibbons, and our President George W. Bush. Fortunately, they have a former president they can look to for answers—Richard Milhous Nixon—you know, the evil president who ended the draft. Not only did President Nixon give my sons the liberty to serve their country by choice, but he also gave a measure of fiscal liberty to the states. He initiated federal revenue sharing. We need revenue sharing now. The federal government has an effective mechanism for collecting taxes from the people. That money can be automatically returned to the states as it is being collected. The states can then spent it to meet their needs. The money is especially needed to pay costs for mandated federal programs. Revenue sharing kept the fox away from state treasuries during the 1970s, it is the answer for state fiscal problems in the first decade of the new century. Richard Nixon, where are you when we need you?

Golden Rule Number Three: He who makes the rules, should provide the gold.

—November 26, 2002

Chapter 20. Good Taxes and a Bad One

Taxes are the price we pay for liberty. But there are good taxes and bad taxes. A good tax produces revenue, it is easy to understand, and it distributes equitable burdens to everyone—after all, liberty is for everyone. A good tax imposes pain. Everyone must participate in the onerous task of paying taxes, lest we not care about the effectiveness, or fairness of government.

Governor Guinn's Tax Committee recommended a broad-based, cover-everyone gross receipts tax. A tax of one-fourth of one percent on all business receipts. This is an income tax—as it will be imposed upon all receipts, ergo income, and it is a sales tax as sales bring receipts. It will be a sales tax on food and drugs. As an income tax and sales tax on food and drugs it probably violates our constitution. So while the tax has the good qualities of producing revenue, the tax money may not be available for over four years—the time necessary to change the state constitution.

I mentioned the gross receipts tax to my graduate students in Public Administration. One asked, "What is this anyway, what do they mean by gross receipts?" He was an educated intelligent public servant, and he was confused. I am too, and I have a Ph.D. The tax is not easy to understand, and when it comes to administering the tax with equity, its comprehension disappears all together.

As soon as the Committee recommended a gross receipts tax, the expected litany of verbiage followed. Everyone would be included, but then there would be an exemption of $350,000 to help small businesses, so one-half the businesses wouldn't pay anything, and other businesses might pay different rates because their bottomline margins could vary, and while non-profitable businesses might pay the full tax, non-profit business organizations—like labor unions and churches were exempt. No wonder unions are beating the drums for this tax. Gaming is too. Surprise? The gross tax becomes a net tax for casinos. Get this, a grocery store will pay a tax on all money paid into the store when customers buy food. There will be no consideration for the cost the store paid for the food. But casinos will pay the tax on all money placed into gaming machines BUT ONLY AFTER the cost of the prizes given to the player is deducted. In other words, for gaming the gross receipts tax is a gross net receipts tax, or a net gross receipts tax. Yeah, me too, I'm confused.

Any tax that is broad-based tax, and good for all, should not be accompanied by exemptions, exceptions, and special applications for special interests.

We need new taxes, but good ones. The gross receipts tax is a bad tax. Its worse quality is that its impacts will be passed onto unsuspecting consumers who will be paying but not feeling the pain. At least with sales taxes, the pain is put in our faces when we buy goods.

Don't tax you, don't tax me, tax the fellow behind the tree. Too often in Nevada we accept the notion that others should pay our taxes for us. Those proposing taxes should participate in paying the taxes they propose. It is time we pay our own taxes, we are the battle born state and we should be reach into our pockets and pay for our battle born liberties.

—December 3, 2002

Chapter 21. Everyone (Me Too) Should Pay Taxes

Everyone should pay taxes.

Everyone should pay taxes: the richest casino executive, the homeless man living in the Las Vegas wash, and Bill Thompson too.

The Spanish Dictator Francisco Franco came to power after a civil war. He was brutal, and half the people hated him. How could he rule? Easy. He announced that the people would not pay taxes. No income tax, no sales tax, no property tax. Half the people still hated him, but they tolerated his oppression. After all, if they revolted, they might get a nice ruler who would tax them.

Of course, they paid taxes indirectly, as businesses paid taxes, and they paid higher prices. But they didn't feel the pain of taxes. They didn't care about government.

If all the people in Nevada cared about the government as much as casino interests that pay heavy taxes, then maybe all the people could be represented on committees the governor appoints to determine our public policies.

Recommendation One: The sales tax should apply to all tangible goods sold in Nevada. Yes, food and drugs too. No loopholes. If the sales tax were a broad based tax on every sale, then the tax could be lowered to five cents or maybe four cents, and it would still bring in extra revenue. When the current fiscal crisis abates with growth in the economy this admittedly regressive tax could be lowered to three cents or two cents on the dollar.

The taxation system should be simple. A one sales tax to fit all, satisfies this principle. So too would my second recommendation: a surtax charge added to federal income taxes. This tax would satisfy another principle: taxes should impose a greater burden on those who can afford greater burdens.

This surcharge or piggyback tax is used today in Rhode Island and Vermont. Individual and business taxpayers take their federal income tax bill, add a percentage to it, and send the extra money to the state. Consider Nevada. This past year individuals and businesses paid about 9 billion dollars to the federal I.R.S.. If we added a 3% surcharge, the state would realize an additional $270 million dollars. Coupled with sales tax gains, adjustments in cigarette taxes and gaming taxes, the state could balance its budget, and meet the service needs of the citizens. The beauty of a surcharge tax is that the state would not have to develop rules regarding income taxes, and the state would not have to set up its own I.R.S. We would simply accept the federal rules, and add a percentage. We might even ask the I.R.S. to collect the surcharge for us, and sent the money to Carson City.

While there is a state constitutional prohibition on personal income taxes, the state constitution might have to be changed for this tax. On the other hand, the courts could accept the tax on a temporary basis and call it a tax not on income, but rather a tax on our income tax bills. If we wanted an immediate tax return without court challenges, we could temporarily impose a 20% charge on business income tax returns. This would give us the same revenue. Those who pay gaming taxes, would have the surcharges credited to those taxes.

These are two ideas based on solid taxation principles. They were not considered by the governor's panel of elite Nevadans. Everyone should pay taxes. These are my ideas for taxes that I would pay.

—December 18, 2002

Everyone.

Chapter 22. Caesars: Render Unto Carson City

On a most special day long ago, a humble man and a perfect woman ended a long overland journey to Bethlehem. The journey was necessitated by a decree that a census be taken so that the Romans could impose a head tax on residents of a colonial outpost. A head tax does satisfy one principle of taxation—everyone pays. But then, the poor pay the same as the rich and that isn't good. A taxation system should offer a blend of taxes each of which meets some principle of good taxation, but ones that collectively produce the needed revenues for government. We cannot overlook gambling taxes. They are very important. About 40% of the state's budget comes from the gaming win tax.

First, let me offer a recommendation that we have a limited state lottery. Our casinos should be authorized to sell multi-state Powerball lotto tickets. These sales could result in an additional $50 million for the state. And the casinos would realize a 7% fee as ticket agents. Only lotto tickets however, as that is the only lottery game Nevadans want. The neat thing about this is that if the sales are in the unrestricted casinos they need not be considered lotteries—as keno and bingo games—also lotteries—are simply considered casino games. Moreover this is one revenue source that can be adopted by a simple majority vote of the legislature, it is not a "tax."

My second recommendation will send chills up the spines of casino executives—but I hope they listen. I am happy that our state has low gaming taxes, and I want it that way—low taxes encourage the mega-resort developments that keep us the gambling capital of the world. However, we should have one, and only one gaming tax rate. The gaming win tax should be set at 8% for all gaming—in big casinos, in small casinos, in bars and taverns, in grocery stores. The gaming tax is like other taxes, it is passed onto the consumers, and there is no reason to treat one gambling customer any different than another one for tax purposes. Moreover, it is absurd to favor smaller casinos over big ones. Their owners are not "mom and pop"—they are wealthy people, and quite frankly this town needs bigger casinos not smaller ones. And our taxes should not encourage more tavern and grocery store gambling. No grocery store, tavern or small casino invites in high rollers with free plane tickets and a bevy of expensive comps for all sorts of pleasures.

What Should Gambling Pay?

While this would be an increase in casino taxes—now set at 6 1/4th %, I would recommend that all other game fees (state and local)—fees per machine, per table, per employee—be eliminated in casinos. Just one tax. Of course, the grocery stores and taverns would have to have their gaming machines linked to a central reporting computer, but then the statewide machines of Louisiana, South Dakota, Oregon and elsewhere are so linked together.

Why 8%—it is the magical number—it is the basic gaming tax paid by casinos of New Jersey—our number two casino state—and by

Mississippi and South Dakota, the number three and five casino states in terms of the number of facilities. No longer would casinos have to answer the truly embarrassing question—"why are you willing to pay more elsewhere?" The 8%, if applied as a single gaming tax, would probably represent about a one per cent increase in gaming taxes, and hey, the increase could be offset to a degree by new revenues from Powerball ticket sales. The tax would yield the state an additional $100 million a year.

If Joseph and Mary could go the extra mile to pay their head taxes to the Romans, our casinos can also render unto Carson City a bit more for the privileges Carson City has rendered unto the casinos.

—December 24, 2002

Chapter 23. Capitalism and Nevada Power

I love capitalism. I rejoiced when Maggie Thatcher privatized Britain, when the Berlin Wall fell, and when Makhail Gorbachev and Boris Yeltsin ushered socialism out of Russia. It seems if you want to find a communist nowadays, you have to go to Berkeley, Boulder, or Eugene. But now the opponents of capitalism are making their move on Las Vegas—heretofore a bastian of conservative economic thought. Or are they?

Our largest government owned corporation—the Las Vegas Water Authority—is seeking to public-ize the region's largest private business—Nevada Power—a subsidiary of Sierra Pacific Resources. The Water Authority is trying to purchase the private utility for 3.2 billion dollars.

Is this the first strike in a communist counter revolution? Does this represent a frontal attack on capitalism? Let's think about it.

Capitalism is a system of production and distribution activities with mutual and even synergistic benefits for all involved. Profits are made for owners when goods are made and sold to customers who could not otherwise obtain the quality goods at reasonable low prices. A Win-Win game.

Capitalism operates in a free market environment where consumers can choose the owners from whom they purchase products.

So let's query the status of capitalism if private Nevada Power succumbs to the purchasing bid by the public Water Authority.

Does Nevada Power represent capitalism? First of all, we must recognize that Nevada Power is a monopoly. There is no free market place, consumers do not have a free choice regarding suppliers. If consumers want power, for the most part, they are stuck with Nevada Power.

Hoover Dam Nevada knows about public ownership of Electricity.
(Courtesy Special Collections, UNLV)

But what about the other important elements of capitalism? Remember, an essential point of capitalism is to bring profits to owners while delivering quality goods to consumers at the acceptable lowest possible prices. But with Nevada Power it is not working this way. Instead of achieving profits, their owners are looking at bankruptcy on the horizon. Stock prices have plummeted over 60% in the past year. And the customers are fully aware that even with lower quality goods—electricity subject to brown-outs—the price of power has skyrocketed.

Management of Nevada Power is simply not being capitalistic as it seems to have the greatest concern for management—not owners, not customers. Sound familiar. Management cares not for owners when it categorically rejects a Water Authority offer that would pay owners $12 for stock now worth only $6 a share. Management cares not for customers when it rejects new ownership mechanisms that would lower power prices.

O.K. So much for Nevada Power, what about the Las Vegas Water Authority and capitalism? The Water Authority, like Nevada Power is a monopoly provider. It does not operate with free markets. But consider these points. The owners of the Water Authority are the public. They are receiving profits from their ownership. Indeed, the profits are so great that the Water Authority commands resources that allow it to offer $3.2 billion to purchase Nevada Power. The Water Authority is being run for the benefit of the customers too. High quality water is being sold to the consumers at low prices. The Water Authority managers are not just serving themselves at the sacrifice of the owners and the consumers. Indeed, the structure of management makes them directly responsible to both the owners—the public—and the customers—the public. They are responsibly subject to public control through political processes. The managers of Nevada Power have shown no such responsibility.

Nonetheless, Nevada Power objects to the purchase offer as they bemoan the notion that the Water Authority lacks experience to operate the Power Company. But the experience the Water Authority lacks is the experience of facing bankruptcy, the experience of not caring about owners, the experience of not caring about customers.

The Water Authority does not have experience in providing high costs and low quality. We must agree—they do not share the experience of Nevada Power.

What the Las Vegas Water Authority does demonstrate is experience in delivering the benefits of capitalism. Nevada Power does not.

No, we are not witnessing a communist counter revolution that our friends in Boulder and Eugene can celebrate. The take-over effort is a victory for capitalism, and I love capitalism.

—October 1, 2002

Chapter 24. Have a Joint, Save Your Grocery Store

I want to save Raley's. It is my favorite grocery store. However, recently I was in Raley's, and many shelves were empty. There were rumors the store might close. Kroger's may take over Raley's. I worry. Guess what? My worries are about to end. We have a solution. Nevadans will soon be able to vote for Proposition 9. We can legalize marijuana for use in our homes.

Just think: our collective society will soon be toking-up, and we soon will be hungry all the time. Everyone will be running to Raley's to buy more and more food. The store's profits will soar. Raley's will survive.

If the proponents of Proposition 9 would just think of our local grocery stores, they might have some persuasive arguments for their measure. But alas, they retreat to the old argument. They claim that if we legalize other things that are bad—or even worse—such as alcoholic beverages or, heaven forbid, gambling—then we are hypocrites if we do not legalize something else that is bad—albeit maybe not as bad—marijuana.

While the supposition regarding which of the substances is worse may be debatable, the line of reasoning is not. It is a stupid line of reasoning.

I believe that before Nevada latches on to another bad substance, before we give our collective social approval to something else that is harmful, we should demonstrate at least a modicum of successful experience regulating the other harmful substances—in this case gambling and alcoholic beverages. What is our record? Have we done a good job with control?

First, let us look at gambling. Wide-open casino gambling began in 1931. Our regulation efforts are now successful in keeping almost all of the bad guys out of the industry, and the games are honest. But in a few areas we could do better with regulation—keeping children away from the games, and we could treat compulsive gamblers—not to "comps," but toward recovery. But overall, I'd give the state a B plus, or maybe A minus.

How about our control of alcoholic beverages? We are one of a few places in America that allows the sale of alcoholic beverages 24 hours a day. And we do not hold the sellers of the beverages responsible at all for the actions of the drunks they keep drunk. We also allow public drinking in places where minors are present.

Two recent experiences of mine found me in the Reno airport and also at a UNLV football game. At the airport, an intoxicated man was wandering about the gate area with a large cup of beer in his hands. I was not comfortable waiting for my plane and thinking I might be sharing the friendly skies with a drunk.

At the recent football game, I witnessed a parade of Metro police officers going time after time into different sections of the crowd pulling out drunks that were bothering sober fans. For most, UNLV football is a sobering experience. The drunks purchase their beer at the stadium and they drink it in the stands. It is actually sold in the stands. Not a good strategy for building up attendance at local sports events. Of course, we put the stadium ten miles away so that none of these drunks can walk home—they all drive home.

It is no surprise that Nevada leads the nation in drunk driving arrests and in drunk driving deaths. That's our record regulating alcoholic beverages. I'd give the state a D minus on its efforts.

Are we ready to legalize and regulate marijuana use? If we could regulate the use as well as we regulate gambling, we might give it a go. But then we should also remember that it took us 30 years to get the regulation of gambling right, and in those thirty years, we did have the Mob, and we did have a lot of dishonest games. We have been at the alcohol control game since 1933, and we still haven't gotten it right.

So are we really ready to regulate marijuana use? While I ponder that question, this time I will pass. I will just say "No" on Proposition 9.

—October 23, 2002

(Writer's Note: Proposition was defeated, and alas Raley's did close).

25. Three Heart Beats Away

The United States Senate has an opportunity to start the New Year off right. With new leadership.

Lott's out, Frist's in as Republican majority leader. Nevadans can cheer that Harry Reid may soon be minority leader.

This will be the highest post a Nevadan has held in the Senate since Key Pittman reigned as President Pro Tempore. That's a position to think about.

In the whole Strom Thurmond—Trent Lott Imbroglio, we totally overlooked the fact that Thurmond—with his baggage—segregation, infirmities of old age—served as the President Pro Tempore for 13 of the past 22 years. As President Pro Tempore he was, in accordance with the Succession Act of 1947, three heart beats away from being the president. He was third in line to the White House behind President Reagan—who suffered an assassination attempt, Bush the 41st, and Speaker Tip O'Neil—a cancer victim.

The Republicans put Thurmond in that position, but we can't let the Democrats off the hook, no matter how much they like to point fingers.

Let's think back to July 28, 1972. On that day the Democrat majority of the U.S. Senate unanimously selected a new President Pro Tempore. So who did the company of McGovern, Kenndey, Muskie, Humphrey, Ervin, and Nevada's Howard Cannon and Alan Bible pick? None other than Senator James Eastland of Mississippi.

Eastland was an outspoken champion of segregation. He had previously addressed a White Citizens Council saying, "When in the course of human events it becomes necessary to abolish the Negro race, proper methods should be used. Among these are guns, bows and arrows, slingshots and knives..." He had not changed his views by 1972. He was an ardent supporter of George Wallace for President.

The Democrats with the rest of us cringed at Senator Lott's recent remarks. Now the Democrats did not make favorable remarks about a James Eastland presidency. No. What did they do? They put him in the direct line of succession to the actual presidency. Three heart beats away.

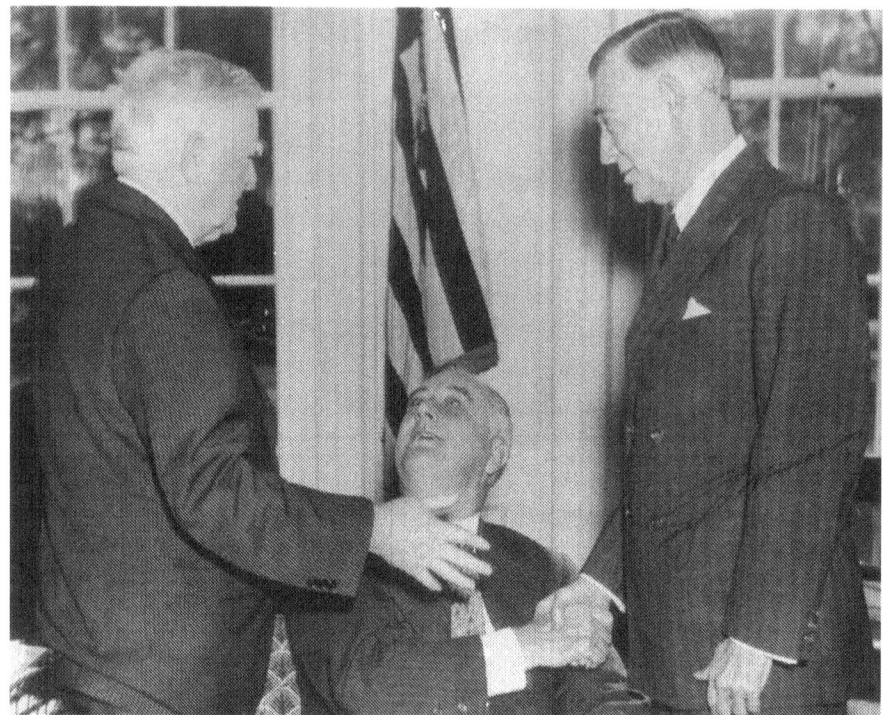

President Pro Tempore Nevada's Senator Key Pittman (right) with President Roosevelt and Vice President Garner.

And from 1972 to 1979 who stood in front of Senator Eastland keeping him from the White House? Vice President Agnew—oops, he resigned. Two heart beasts away. A President named Nixon, oops, another resignation. One heart beat away. A Strong heart. No! Our third line of defense against James Eastland actually becoming president of the United States of America was Speaker of the House Carl Albert, a man who had previously suffered a massive heart attack. We survived—why have we forgotten?

Before The Democrats chose Eastland as President Pro Tempore, they selected Senators Alan Ellender of Louisiana, George of Georgia, Russell of Georgia, and our own Pittman. Afterwards, they selected Stennis of Mississippi, and Robert Byrd of West Virginia, a former member of the Ku Klux Klan who still uses the "N" word in public.

In this day of world terrorism we must have in the line of succession persons capable of being president. The Senate will soon select a new President Pro Tempore. Let's break with the tradition of selecting the most senior bigot to be three heart beats away. Let the Republicans and Democrats get together and select a Senator who has shown leadership and an ability to command national respect. My candidates are Senators John McCain and Joe Lieberman—a selection of the latter would introduce a much needed sense of bipartisanship to the body.

We should celebrate Harry Reid's new celebrity, but we must urge our Senators Reid and Ensign to use their brains on this one. If they cannot do so, then please pass a law taking the post of President Pro Tempore out of the line of succession to the Presidency.

—December 31, 2002

Chapter 26. A Preview of Volume 2: The HNN Essays: The Ironies of a Nuclear State

(Note: In volume 2 of <u>Parables from (a not quite) Paradise, NV 89154</u>, the author will present a series of essays that were published in the e-journal <u>HistoryNewsNetwork.org</u>. The essays will focus upon national and international themes. One of the themes—nuclear waste disposal—overlapped in content with the KNPR commentaries presented here in volume 1. As a preview of volume 2, two essays are presented here. The first deals with the nuclear ironies of Nevada, a state that welcomed almost everything—except waste—that was nuclear prior to—and even after—the emergence of the nuclear waste issue, while the second treats the historical issue of "nullification" in the context of nuclear waste policy.)

For the last 70 years, Nevada has been neither a Democrat state nor a Republican state. It has consistently been the gambling state. The voters—only a handful of whom have been born in the state, have tolerated—and voted for—both very liberal and very conservative candidates for state and federal office. Taking their cues from a gambling industry which invests heavily in political campaigns, the voters have never tolerated candidates who show independence or weakness vis-a-vis the real "party line," ergo, the full-fledged support of casino gambling, as determined by the casino industry.

But now the state has a new bottomline "critical issue." Now all aspiring politicians must rally around another cause as well. They must be willing to "go to the mat" to show that they oppose having nuclear waste brought to the state and put into a repository at Yucca Mountain, 100 miles northwest of Las Vegas. "No Nuclear Waste," and "Nevada is not a Wasteland," have become the battle cries of our public leaders and also of our populace.

There are many ironies regarding the new rigid stance taken by the state. The first irony concerns the vehemence with which the leaders and followers seek to protect "their" land, and the vehemence with which they cry out that "Nevada has already done its share," for the nation. What does "our" land mean, anyway? Not one of the five most recent governors of Nevada was born in the state. Only 6% of the adults of southern Nevada (Las Vegas and surrounding Clark

County) were born in the state. Statewide, 13% of the population is native born, the smallest percentage among all 50 states. The average resident of southern Nevada came to the state (or was born in the state) in 1991. Yet majorities loudly protest that the waste which may be placed in "our" desert lands 100 miles away will destroy "our" quality of life, to say nothing about destroying the influx of tourist dollars to Las Vegas. We do get 36 million visitors per year.

Very few of the new residents, and almost none of the tourists has ever driven by the lands where the waste may be stored. The lands are miles away from the road running 450 miles to Carson City, Tahoe and Reno, and most people going that way fly. We are simply not familiar with "our" lands.

A second irony concerns the lands with which we are familiar—lands within the Las Vegas metropolitan area. Here we almost categorically refuse to take ownership over "quality of life" issues. There is almost zero political or public outcry about the many social maladies that beset us—high school drop out rates, teen age pregnancies and suicides, adult suicides, smoking and cancer deaths, drunk driving incidents, child abuse and child abuse deaths, myriad addictions including, of course, compulsive gambling. All these factors find Nevada among the nation's leaders (on the wrong side of the equation). Yet no casino dollar has been given to a candidate in order to make an appeal that might address these "problems" for "our" land. The nuclear waste issue also preempts concerns about the real crises of high malpractice insurance rates prompting doctors to leave Las Vegas, and also the minimal numbers of nurses in the state—the lowest number per capita in America. (LVRJ, February 24, 2001; March 6, 2002).

A third irony concerns the notion of "ownership" of the desert lands and the desires to keep the lands free of nuclear contaminants and the political history of the state. The actions of politicians (acting with public support) over the years since 1930 (around when full casino gambling was legalized throughout the state) belie concerns for a clean earth policy. The politicians and then-residents of the state eagerly sought out federal selection for a variety of military and defense projects including ones involving nuclear energy and nuclear weapons. Federal military-related programs are the second biggest sector of the state economy.

Hawthorne had 250 residents in 1920 and it was headed toward becoming another Nevada ghost town. However, a disaster at a New Jersey Navy ammunition depot presented an opportunity. U.S. Senator Tasker Oddie and Representative Samuel Arentz (both of Nevada) persuaded the Department of War to place a new ammunition facility in the dry desert terrain of Hawthorne. Now an Army ammunition site, the depot still provides the economic basis for the small city. (Hulse, The Silver State, 1991, pp. 333-5).

Hawthorne Ammunition Depot

The Army Air Corps placed a training facility just north of Las Vegas in 1942. After World War Two state political leaders including the late Howard Cannon used their seniority to have Nellis Air Force Base made the essential jet flight training school as well as air gunnery (live fire) range for our military. Cannon also worked hard for the placement of an MX missile defense system in the state, but on that score he did not have universal support among the population, albeit many in Las Vegas were counting the dollars expected to come with a real estate boom and 100,000 new residents. Other air stations have been placed near Reno, in Fallon and at Wendover, on the Utah state border. (Hulse, pp.214-5, 271).

At the conclusion of World War Two a program of testing nuclear weapons began on several Pacific Ocean islands. However, logistics made planning and execution of the tests somewhat inconvenient. In 1950 President Truman secretly planned to move the tests to a site within the United States. A site adjacent to the Nellis gunnery range at Yucca Flats in the Nevada desert was selected. The first atmospheric bomb test was made on January 27, 1951. From then until atmospheric tests were finally stopped in December 1962 (and banned by a treaty in August 1963), over 100 bombs were dropped above the ground. Between 1963 and 1993 about 800 more tests were conducted underground. (In all there were 928 tests in Nevada). However, nuclear materials were vented into the atmosphere in at least 200 cases with underground tests, with some of these tests propelling nuclear particles off of the test site. (LeBaron, America's Nuclear Legacy, 1998, p. 70).

While the selection of the site was made in secret, it cannot be said that the decision was opposed by Nevadans. Powerful U. S. Senator Patrick McCarran supported the move entirely, as did residents who saw the Nevada Test Site as a great source of economic benefit for the state. UNLV Political Scientist A. C. (Dina) Titus wrote in her University of Nevada Press book Bombs in the Backyard (1986), "...the southern Nevada papers strongly endorsed the testing program, presenting the public with positive headlines and patriotic editorials...state officials at every level were eager to accommodate the needs of the new facility which brought in federal dollars." She added that press coverage "failed to address more serious questions about the possible harmful effects of fallout." (p. xiii).

Residents did not protest. Instead they held parties at the edge of the city from whence they could see the flash of a nuclear blast, and if they were "lucky" they could view the mushroom cloud. Indeed, a fiery nuclear cloud was the symbol found on the Clark County official seal in the 1950s. Casinos held promotional events tied to the explosions. In 1957, the Sands, home of the "Rat Pack," held a "Miss Atomic Bomb" contest with the winner decked out in a scantily-sized bathing suit which was shaped like a mushroom cloud. (Titus, p. 93).

Nevadans found nuclear tests to be desirable.
(Courtesy Special Collections, UNLV)

The Atomic Queen of Nevada: Good for the Economy
(Courtesy of Special Collections, UNLV)

The same year, according to Titus (p. 97), the Nevada state senate passed resolutions asking the federal government to "build an experimental nuclear-power generating plant" in the state, and also to use the Naval Ammunition Depot at Hawthorne to store "nonconventional weapons."

The residents downwind from the atmospheric tests, most of whom lived in Utah, were not as "lucky." Actually the American public has not been lucky. One federal study reveals that it is likely that nuclear weapons tests have caused at least 15,000 cancer deaths in the United States. (USA Today, February 28, 2002).

To be sure, the negative effects of the nuclear radiation were not fully addressed. Perhaps now the political establishment is making up for that early neglect with its rigid "no waste" policy. However, by the

1950s the effects of radiation poisoning were known, and certainly results of the atmospheric "tests" over Hiroshima and Nagasaki were rather public.

In 1984 when presidential candidate Gary Hart stated that he would seek a moratorium on underground testing, Nevada organized labor immediately attacked him. His Nevada campaign headquarters disavowed the stance. In 1992 state political leaders, while already nearly unanimous in opposition to the placing of even low level nuclear waste in Nevada, stepped forth to protest the stopping of underground nuclear tests, and they lobbied hard to make sure the Test Site itself was not closed down. At its peak time of operations the Nevada Test Site facilities did provide employment (with support jobs) for over 18,000 Nevadans. (Titus, 68, 100).

Alas when underground tests were stopped, Nevada officials sought more nuclear projects for the state. In 1995, the state's two U.S. Senators, Harry Reid and Richard Bryan both protested when Savannah River, South Carolina was selected over the Nevada Test Site to have a multi-billion dollar radioactive gas production plant. "This is one of the types of things that gives Congress the bad name it now has," Reid opined. Bryan added, "This is abominable public policy." They claimed that Nevada lost the nuclear project because of "pork barreling." (Las Vegas Review Journal, August 5, 1995).

In 1996 the state's congressional delegation also protested when Congress determined that tests at the site would be permanently banned. Senator Reid sought an amendment allowing the president to authorize a test on his own when he deemed it necessary. Reid was roundly criticized by Nevada environmentalists and groups such as Greenpeace for his actions seeking continued testing. (LVRJ, June 27, 1996).

As an aside, in November 1997, the Nevada legislature passed a resolution asking the Smithsonian Institute to return the Enola Gay, the plane from which the atomic bomb was dropped on Hiroshima, to Wendover, Nevada, where it was located before flying to Tinian Island and then Japan. The legislature thought it would be a wonderful exhibit to use to attract tourists to the desert town. Things we like to celebrate! No wonder Halloween is a state holiday. (LVRJ, November 14, 1997).

The Mercury, Nevada Testing Facility: nuclear tests meant jobs.
(Courtesy Special Collections, UNLV)

By the 1980s the nation had 78 Nuclear energy facilities. Waste materials were beginning to be amassed at each of the sites.

The waste is now stored in cooling ponds at the reactor sites. However if the ponds become filled, the waste will have to be in above the ground dry containers. The manner of storage in both cases is not totally secure. The waste materials are subject to weather disturbances (tornados and floods), as well as earthquakes and even volcanic eruptions. The events of September 11 also raise concerns that the multiplicity of sites would be more vulnerable to sabotage. That thinking was also present in 1982 when Congress passed the Nuclear Waste Policy Act. The act provided for the creation of a waste storage site by 1998. The site would be paid for by taxes on the nuclear facilities. At first three potential sites would be selected and studied for feasibility. Then the president would pick one of the sites, after which the host state's governor could veto the plan. The veto could be overturned by majority votes in both houses of congress. Sites in Washington State and in Texas were studied along with

Yucca Mountain, Nevada. However in a new action, Congress in 1987 passed an act that limited study to the single site at Yucca Mountain. Political leaders in Nevada called this law, not affectionately, the "Screw Nevada" Law. In 1989, the law was changed again, this time putting a date of 2010 for the opening of the waste facility. (Los Angeles Times, January 29, 1995).

In February (2002), President Bush selected Yucca Mountain to be the site. Nearly $7 billion had been spent in scientific and other studies of the site. Bush also indicated his choice was based upon concerns about terrorism at the scattered nuclear power facilities. Soon afterwards, Nevada Governor Kenny Guinn vetoed the plan. We now are awaiting action by Congress. Congress has 90 days to override the veto. (LVRJ, February 16, 2002; New York Times, March 9, 2002).

Politics or Science? The answer has to be a simple one: Politics. There is no way to measure the terrorism factor with scientific accuracy. Placement of all waste at Yucca Mountain will afford great security. However, the risky question persists: is it better to keep nuclear waste at 78 power plants (and other military sites) in 39 states, or is it better to transport the materials thousands of miles through 42 states on its journeys to Nevada? Right now, the September 11 fear mentality seeks to reduce the number of major targets, and individual trucks or rail cars carrying waste are not viewed as major targets, albeit many precautions will be taken over the transportation routes.

The Nevada response points to scientific questions about possible long term (measured in hundreds or thousands of years) leakage of materials into water tables in the desert, and also to risks of transportation sabotage or accidents. However, the "group think" psychology of Nevada politics sees voters responding positively to rigid political positions against "all" nuclear waste materials. "Political" has to be the conclusion considering the continuing record of the state's support for nuclear testing activity. The same political leaders that are quick to point out how the state has already made its sacrifices (in having politically acceptable and economically beneficial military facilities and nuclear testing facilities), now point to great damage that will be done to the state, its reputation (?), and its citizens' health by having waste stored in the state. They have riled up a population that is quite blaze about social maladies in their neighborhoods to be quite angry about degradation of desert lands that a few years ago were the sites for atmospheric and underground nuclear blasts.

To be sure, this writer absolutely does not want nuclear trucks or rail cars moving through the populated Las Vegas metropolitan area. At the same time he would like to see some political concern for the social pollution and the impending medical services crisis in our populated communities as well. And that view, consistent with long standing views in Nevada politics, is neither Democrat nor Republican.

—History News Network, March 25, 2002

Chapter 27: A Preview of Volume 2: The HNN Essays: Nullification—Latest Round

The annals of federal-state relationships have been punctuated by several episodes of state efforts to nullify federal executive actions. In the past these efforts have been essentially extra legal (and/or illegal), and they have been unsuccessful. A contemporary nullification fight—one going on at this very moment—is different. It is taking place under the guise of federal law according to procedures set down in words by the national congress. The effort will, however, end the same, it will fail.

The current effort of state nullification of federal executive action will, on the other hand, be a successful one if it wins support of a single house of congress. The processes of this nullification campaign are convoluted, to say the least. Whichever way the matter is concluded after congressional action, the fight will continue in federal courts with a constitutional challenge of those processes.

Today's nullification battle is the fourth such battle in our nation's constitutional history. The three previous fights included South Carolina's attempt to repudiate enforcement of federal tariff policy in 1832, the collective effort of eleven southern states to block federal enforcement of laws during the Civil War Era of 1861-1865, and the efforts of many of the same states to interpose their authority on behalf of their citizens against implementation of federal policies mandating racial integration of schools in the 1950s and 1960s.

The government of South Carolina was convinced that the 1828 and 1832 national tariff acts which called for high protective tariffs on manufactured goods were designed to assist northern industry to the strong detriment to its own agricultural interests. The acts were also seen as an attack upon the economic viability of the institution of slavery. Leaders in South Carolina protested the federal efforts by calling a state convention which passed resolutions indicating that the tariffs would not be imposed at ports of entry into the state. The strongly worded resolutions indicated the state would use force to support its cause.

President Andrew Jackson found that the state actions precluded any opportunity for compromise. Although he was a states' rights advocate and he was born in South Carolina, Jackson responded in kind. He mobilized troops and he ordered them to South Carolina if the state resisted implementation of the tariff provisions. Congress supported his moves. South Carolina backed down. In the process, its leading politician, John C. Calhoun, resigned his position as Vice President of the United States. In 1833, the Great Compromiser, Henry Clay, maneuvered a bill through Congress which made the episode less onerous for South Carolina. The state repealed its nullification proclamation. The 1833 tariff act gradually rolled back tariff rates to pre-1828 schedules.

The results of the next nullification episode were not as peaceful. In 1861 South Carolina nullified the constitution and all federal law enforcement in its borders. South Carolina was followed by ten other states, and the Civil War ensued. This failed case study in nullification is amply recorded in tens of thousands of books.

Post Civil War compromises on the enforcement of certain federal provisions (constitutional and statutory) in the states formerly in rebellion allowed the states to impose illegal (in effect, if not in word) policies of racial segregation in public facilities. The state policies mandating public separation of races were ruled unconstitutional in 1954 by the United States Supreme Court. The next year the Court issued rulings regarding the immediate implementation of national policies for integration.

The governors of the states with policies of segregation began a pattern of resistance to the decisions. Supported by their state legislatures, governors such as Ross Barnett of Mississippi, Orval Faubus of Arkansas, and George Wallace of Alabama orchestrated the policy of interposition. The governors soon found themselves "standing in the school house door" blocking federal enforcement agents from accompanying African American students into previously all-white schools. At the school sites the governors would be flanked by the commanders of their state national guard along with troops of the guard. The guard would represent a show of force against federal action. But inevitably, it was but a show. As if by prearrangement, in each case the president would proclaim that the state national guard was to called into federal service and placed under command of the U.S. Army. The "Army" would in turn leave the governor's side and support the actions of the federal agents. Interposition and other legalistic efforts to resist policies of integration did slow down implementation, but national policy prevailed.

The fourth nullification episode is the first one to take place outside of the South. (An 1812 Hartford Convention advocated nullification, but this was a meeting of Federalist Party politicians not government officials). The current episode was prompted, the better word would be "created," by the Nuclear Waste Policy Act of 1982. The Act provided that the federal government (Department of Energy) would study sites for storing nuclear waste materials generated by power plants (and other facilities) in 42 states. After the study was completed, the Secretary of Energy would recommend one site for storing nuclear waste underground.

The president would then accept or reject the site. If the president agreed with the selection, he would inform the state where the site was located, that he had made his selection. The governor of the state would then have 60 days in which to veto the action of the president. If there was no veto, action on developing the site would begin. However, if, as expected, the governor vetoed the president's action, the veto could be overridden only if both houses of congress voted to over ride (by majority vote) the veto within ninety days. If but one house supported the governor, the governor's veto of the president's action would be confirmed. The process of selecting a nuclear waste site would have to begin anew.

The 1982 Act also indicated that the Department of Energy would start its study by looking at sites in Texas, Washington State, and Nevada. In 1987, another act of congress limited the study of potential sites to the Yucca Mountain site in Nevada. On February 14, 2002, after fifteen years of study costing the federal government over 12 billion dollars, Secretary of Energy Spencer Abraham recommended the Yucca Mountain site for storage of nuclear waste. On February 15, 2002, President George W. Bush selected the Yucca Mountain site. As expected, on April 9, 2002, Nevada Governor Kenny Guinn vetoed the action of the president. This is the first time in American History that a governor has "legally" (I emphasize the quotation marks) vetoed the action of a president. Congress has until July 9, 2002, to sustain or override the veto.

The politics are quite simple. Nevada has four votes in congress, two in the House, two in the Senate. The forty plus states with nuclear waste within their borders (now temporarily stored above ground at the generating sites), have over 400 votes in the House and over 80 votes in the Senate. If they want to keep the waste at the temporary storage areas which are quickly filling up in many cases, they may vote to sustain Governor Guinn's veto. If they fear transporting the waste through their states toward Nevada more than they fear having the waste permanently in their midst, they may also sustain the veto. However, by sustaining the veto they are introducing the possibility of having another waste site, perhaps a site in their own state.

If they vote to override the veto, they are assured that most of the waste will be moved to Nevada (all of the waste will be moved over a timed schedule).

The congressional votes are being lobbied and counted. The nuclear energy generating plants and the power companies want the waste moved to Nevada and they have lobbying funds to support overriding Governor Guinn's veto. The state of Nevada has authorize the expenditure of three million dollars in their campaign to win congressional support for the veto.

Ironically, at the very moment the state of Nevada is waging its costly uphill battle for a nullification victory, the state's Department of Motor Vehicles (DMV) is reconfirming the state's love of everything nuclear. (See March 25 HNN). On April 12, 2002, the DMV announced that the state would be raising money by selling automobile license plates honoring the history of the Nevada atomic bomb testing site at Yucca Flats (adjacent to Yucca Mountain). The new state license plates actually show an atmospheric atomic bomb test. The plate has a mushroom cloud rising through the plate number and encompassing the word "Nevada." The cloud is flanked by a nuclear logo and the formula $e=mc2$. There are estimates that 15,000 Americans died as a result of the atmospheric tests. Nevada likes to talk about the danger of radiation. But the state just can't quite resist celebrating its nuclear past and making a buck off it in the process. I expect the license plates will be issued in time for Senators Reid and Ensign to sport them on their cars in Washington, D.C., as they drive about seeking votes to support Governor Guinn's veto.

The nullification fight will not end in July 2002. The veto arrangement with a governor's action along with support of but one house of congress reversing the executive action of a president was set into the law in 1982. In 1983, the United States Supreme Court ruled in Immigration and Naturalization Service v. Chadha that legislative vetoes of executive branch actions constituted a clear violation of constitutional provisions for the passage of legislation. Congress is supposed to pass legislation and when it is signed by the president, they are done with their role in the process.

Any reasonable reading of Chadha (a 7-2 Supreme Court ruling) would lead to a conclusion that the action by the governor of Nevada and the override actions by Congress are contrary to the Constitution. So, in final analysis, the matter may be settled in the courts.

Nevada leaders have vowed to fight to the end. If the governor's veto is overridden, Nevada will have a case, but it will be a difficult one. The state will be burdened with showing that the unconstitutional veto process in the 1982 Act is so onerous that it voids the entire act, and hence voids the selection of Yucca Mountain for waste storage.

However, in the unlikely event that the governor's veto is sustained, the president will have the easier task of showing only that the provision for the governor's veto and the congressional override is unconstitutional, and that the selection of Nevada for the waste site was validated at the moment the president made the selection.

Either way, the notion of nullification would be negated by a court ruling. And for this Nevadan, that is just as well. What with "quickie" divorces, brothels, grocery store slot machines, Howard Hughes, Meyer Lansky, and Bugsy Siegel, we have enough of a legacy to live with. It would be simply awful if we had to be joined together in the legacy of John C. Calhoun, Ross Barnett, and George Wallace as well.

—History News Network, April 29, 2002

Chapter 28. The Las Vegas Supermarket Casino—My Pet Peeve

In recent years, the Nevada Gaming Commission has focused attention upon locations of restricted license holders. These are places that are permitted to have fifteen or fewer gaming machines. This observer suggests that the policy should be guided by an overriding concern for the public interest of all the citizens of the state of Nevada.

I take this position: the public interest of the state is not served by allowing gambling activities to take place without severe geographical restrictions on locations of gambling; the public interest is not served by prohibiting all commercial gambling activities in the state. Some gambling operations should be encouraged by state policy, others should be strongly discouraged, still others should be outright banned.

The points (1) Both opponents and proponents should agree that some gaming can be in the interest of some communities and society—even if individuals find the activity to be offensive in all its forms. (2) Both opponents and proponents should agree that some forms of gambling are offensive to the community and to society. The opponents should not waste energy condemning all gaming, but rather should seek out the most offensive forms and concentrate attacks on those forms. The proponents should not take the position that all gambling no matter the form is good for society. Instead, the proponents should seek out forms that offer benefits to society and make their defense around those forms.

Religiously I am—like gaming opponent Tom Grey—a Methodist (that is United Methodist). The social creed of my church declares that all gambling is a "menace." This is a Deontological view point—what is wrong is always wrong in whatever form it is packaged. I dissent from the social creed of my church. Rather, I accept a Catholic (catholic?) or Teleological view on the subject of gambling. If an otherwise offensive activity is conducted in a proper way with proper ends, it may be permissible in some forms. This is not a Catholic view of many activities called "sin," but it is the general view regarding

A Nevada Grocery Store Casino.

gambling. If the game is honest, if the players are recreational (not habitual), if the players can play and also meet their other social obligations, and if the bottomline helps the community and society in its pursuit of good things, then the activity MAY be permissible. The Teleological view offers a defense of church bingo. An occasional game is played at low stakes, honestly, and the beneficiary is the local parish, school, food fund, hospital, etc. Permissible. The same can be said of some other charity gambling, some Native American gaming, and maybe also of the Las Vegas Strip. Maybe. Gamblers are recreational tourists (most of them), games certainly are honest, and the end result is a growing economy that provides lots of good entry level jobs for persons who otherwise would not be employed.

Ah! the other side. We have the unregulated slot machine halls of South Carolina which attract pathological gamblers in the middle of the night. It would be hard to successfully apply a Teleological guideline to this kind of gambling operation. The modest tax revenues gained can hardly offset the tremendous potential social harm caused by the activity. Just because it is gambling does not make it good. The authorities in South Carolina are beginning to make the move to eliminate this form of gambling, and the opponents of gambling need to focus their resources in this fight, as that focus can have very positive results for society—a victory for opponents of gambling is very possible in South Carolina.

Gaming advocates should not waste their energies trying to defend slot joints in South Carolina. (Note: South Carolina Machines were forced to stop operations in 2000).

But what about the fight in other states. My state is Nevada. I defend the gaming operations on the Las Vegas Strip. I like the fact that Steve Wynn spends Mirage resources teaching new workers the English language, basic job skills—getting to work on time, personal hygiene, and courtesy. And in the process he makes the Strip the best example of workfare in America. Yet, some local opponents of gambling want to use the Strip as a whipping boy. They see large casinos as some magic cash cow that can be the source of unlimited taxes. Wrong. Taxation will ruin the good things about the Strip. The good things include, jobs, tourism spending that grows an economy, and effective honest gaming operations.

There are some people in Las Vegas who honestly subscribe to the Deontological philosophy. They oppose all gaming activities. Yet, even the most valiant good hearted soul has limited energies to use in order to better society. There is so much to do in society to make it better. We have to be somewhat selective in picking our targets and using our energy. There are better targets than the casinos of the Las Vegas Strip. The targets are right here in our midst. I wish to select just one for consideration. In my mind it is the best target, because it represents the most offensive form of gambling not only in Las Vegas, but anywhere. In my mind it is a target that can be hit in its bull's eye if the full facts about the target can be found and then revealed to the public.

My target is the Video Slot Machines of the Grocery Stores of the Las Vegas Valley. My Catholic view finds that the machines of the grocery stores, while honest (that is, like the machines on the Strip, winners are selected by good random number generators), they attract habitual (or worse) players whose activity reduces their ability to fulfill their obligations to family, community, and society, and in doing so the machines hurt the community and the society. There is no redeeming value achieved to offset the harm caused to local families, community, and society.

However, before I suggest that we pursue any radical policy we need public answers to many questions. If the answers are as I suspect them to be, then the appropriate policy is obvious: take the machines out of the grocery stores. But first, we need answers.

1). What do we know about food store video slot machine players? Who plays these machines? Is the money being played being brought INTO our community? Are the players tourists? How many are tourists? I think the percentage would be somewhere between 0% and 1.29%, but that's just my opinion. Are the players young or old, male or female? I think we would probably find many or most are upper age females. What is their economic situation? Are they affluent like Harrah's casino gambling survey shows the average casino gamblers to be, or are they lower income persons? How many purchase their food with food stamps, before (hopefully) they play?

2). How many of the patrons of supermarket video slot machines are compulsive gamblers? How many of the players at 3 am are compulsives? I think (but just my opinion) that well over half might be designated as problem gamblers, and maybe half as many as compulsives. But that's just my opinion. Let's get the facts.

I might suggest that the Nevada Gaming Commission ask the help of the American Gaming Association in this regard, as the Association has funded a Harvard Medical College study of the subject of compulsive gambling in America.

3). Who is exposed to gambling in the supermarkets of Las Vegas? Answer: everyone. Everyone is not exposed to the Strip gambling, to neighborhood casinos, to bar slot machines to 7-11 slot machines. Why? Because we don't have to go to these places. But guess what: WE HAVE TO EAT, we don't have a choice about going to the market. So (1) Children HAVE TO BE EXPOSED to this gambling—whether we want our children exposed to this gambling or not. Teenagers HAVE TO be exposed to this gambling, whereas our Strip casinos try hard to throw out the teenagers. (2) Recovering addicted gamblers—people in treatment for compulsive gambling— HAVE to have this gambling thrown right into their faces each week when they shop for food. And I dare say we do have more than our share of recovering gamble-holics in Las Vegas. (3) People who want absolutely nothing to do with gambling and gambling people MUST be exposed to this. People are not forced to witness drinking and intoxicated people; they are forced to witness gambling and gambling crazed people—when they go to the store to purchase food for their families. (4) Store employees who wish only to have a job providing a service in selling people the essentials of life—food—must be exposed to gambling. This includes teenagers who find their first jobs in supermarkets.

4). Why must grocery stores in Las Vegas allow smoking at the machines? Is there a state law that gamblers HAVE TO SMOKE? Is this an industry thing to suck more money out of people—like, if they can't smoke, they just might have to walk away from their machine for a break?

The Harvard Medical School should be commissioned by the American Gaming Association to do an intense study of toxic levels of MY FOOD—my produce, my fruits, my food cartons—and MY AIR SPACE—in order to tell me how many carcinogens I am being FORCED to consume so that the supermarkets can make money from the smoking crazed gamblers. I DETEST the notion that stores selling essential goods CAN FORCE ME to expose myself and others to the dangers of CANCER just so they can make some gambling money.

5). Do I receive a better price for food, because of the gambling in grocery stores? When I go to a casino (and I DO) on the Strip, I can enjoy a low cost meal, because the casino is willing to forego its profits on the meal in order to get me into the facility, because, hey, I might just drop a roll of quarters into a machine (and sometimes I DO). Is my grocery bill less because of the video slot machines in the grocery store? We have a store—Luckys—that loves to show us a grocery cart and tell us what the cart of groceries cost at Luckys compared to Smiths, Albertsons, Vons. You know what I want the food store to do? Take their Luckys cart and compare it to the Luckys cart in California, to the Luckys cart in Utah, to the Luckys cart in Arizona. SHOW ME THE MONEY! Show me that I am saving on my Las Vegas groceries because Luckys is sucking out anywhere from $300,000 to $900,000 a year from my neighbors with their video slot machines. I don't think my groceries cost less.

6). And by the way, just how much money do the grocery store machines make? I think WE AS CITIZENS need to know—are the 15 machines (the limit for grocery stores) making an average $30,000 a year, or maybe $40,000, or like one bar $60,000 per machine. Are the machines taxed (they pay a flat fee) an amount more of less than paid by casinos for their slot machines?

7). Where does the money go from the gaming profits on the grocery store video slot machines? To employees? Some—my guess is 5%, but maybe the stores could tell us. To local slot route companies?—Some, my guess is 30%, but what is the truth? TO OUTSIDE CORPORATIONS THAT TAKE THE MONEY OUTSIDE OF MY STATE AND HENCE CONTRIBUTE TO AN ECONOMIC DECLINE IN MY STATE? I think Lots! My guess is 60% or more.

And who are these grocery store owners? Isn't Smiths a Salt Lake City firm? Do they have slot machines in their Salt Lake City markets? Is Albertsons an Idaho firm? Do they allow gambling in their stores in Idaho? Do they sell lottery tickets? Maybe—but do they stay open 24 hours a day just to sell lottery tickets.

Are Vons and Luckys California companies? Didn't one California supermarket chain refuse to sell lottery tickets because it hurt milk sales? Why would such a chain want to sell chances on a video slot machine here?

8). Would the Nevada Gaming Commission support putting video slot machines in bank lobbies? You are considering new locations. A bank lobby would be ridiculous; I think most of us would agree on that. Guess what, each of Las Vegas' supermarket chains has an over-the-counter branch bank in its lobby along with its fifteen slot machines. Not only do we have the entire issue about ATMs nearby (also in every lobby), but BANKS. My ATM will only give me $500 a day—the ATM wants to make sure I will spend my money responsibly. But here I am with my savings book, and its only a few

96

steps away—junior's college fund. Just asking now—but do the banks in the slot machine lobbies inquire about withdrawals and ask if the money is going to go into the slot machines? Do they limit withdrawals over-the-counter to $500 a day? Wouldn't it be appropriate to have questions such as these answered?

Casinos must comply with a myriad of rules when they advance credit to players. They check balances in bank accounts, they look at other assets, they check credit sources. Is it true that the holders of restricted licenses (for 15 slot machines and less) may make casual loans—out of pocket, as it were—to players? I have been told (by a bar operator) that bars may give players up to $10,000 at one time (combined players). Whether it was legal or not, they did so. Is this legal? Do grocery stores do the same? Ever?

The sign beside the machines in one supermarket (Luckys) indicated that checks could be cashed for only up to $100.00. Is this the same policy the supermarket uses for other customers? Is there a state gaming policy on checks in grocery store gambling areas?

9). And why do all the grocery stores have ONLY video machines? Does the Harvard Medical School have the evidence? Aren't these the most addicting gambling devices that may be put in front of a gambler? Haven't problem gambling experts called these machines "electronic morphine" and "the crack cocaine of gambling?" Isn't it true that locals prefer video poker, while tourists prefer reel (spinning figure) slot machines?

10). Now I don't want to stray from supermarket machines, but I do have an inquiry about bar machines. The state rule is that 15 machines (a limited gaming license) can be given only when the gaming will be incidental to other business. Why can't the gaming board ENFORCE that rule? Doesn't it know there are many bars whose machine revenue is greater than their total net revenue—meaning they make money on machines, and LOSE money on everything else. One establishment realized $900,000 from machines, but had net profits for the year of only $600,000. Show me the INCIDENTAL.

Back to supermarkets—can the markets really say that from 12 midnight to 6 am the machines are incidental? Would it be more accurate to say that the SOLE purpose of keeping the grocery stores open at those hours is to serve the cravings of habitual gamblers? I DON'T KNOW! I am just asking.

11). Summary

I think the answers to the questions posed must be forthcoming from the Nevada Gaming Commission if the Commission truly wishes to pursue a policy on restricted slot machine gaming that is in the public interest. If the answers are not as I suspect them to be, perhaps, we can persist in allowing slot machines in grocery stores. If the questions are answered as I suspect they will be, we should begin to set a policy that will lead to the eventual removal of all slot machines from grocery stores.

I would suggest that this removal process could take place over a few years so as not to have a dramatic negative economic impact upon the business owners, albeit it should be recognized that the removal of the machines will probably have a very positive economic impact upon the total community.

The Nevada Gaming Commission can take some immediate steps which do not require intensive studies:

First—Immediately ban smoking in all gaming areas which are open to any areas where food may be exposed to the smoke, or where patrons wishing to purchase food may be exposed to the smoke.

Second—Remove all machines from places where they may be viewed by children.

Third—Require the machine operations to cease for at least several hours each evening.

—-A Presentation to the Nevada Gaming Commission, Carson City, February 26, 1998.

Chapter 29. The Win-Win Game in Las Vegas

Case One: I own two automobiles. I have told many many people about the deal I got on my Jeep. I purchased it used and paid a healthy sum. To be sure I wouldn't have any problems with it, I purchased a warranty for an extra $1,000. Then it broke down. After it was towed into the dealer, I waited, and waited-more than a week. Then I was told the guarantee didn't cover the problem. In frustration I told the dealer to take the Jeep back, and that I didn't want to argue about it. I offered to let him apply what I had paid for it to the sticker price of a new Jeep.

His sales force worked me over real well. The matter ended with the dealer giving me back $2,000 less on the used Jeep toward the price of a new one. I tell everyone about the "deal" I received. As I teach and give speeches, I can say that I have told the story to well in excess of a thousand people. I haven't bothered to tell my story to the dealer, because, quite frankly, I don't want to "deal" with his people again.

My other car? I have driven it coast to coast several times. No problems, 35 miles per gallon, a few oil changes, comfortable. I don't tell people about my other car.

In my research on customer service, I have found that I am typical. Nineteen out of 20 people who have had bad experiences will not bother to take complaints to the provider. They take the complaints to others. They are quick to tell the stories. Each bad commercial experience is told to an average of nine other people. One in five will repeat a losing experience to more than 20 people. Good experiences with merchants are usually told to fewer than five others. Surveys suggest that it takes 12 good stories about a business to outweigh the effects of one bad experience. (Thompson and Comeau, 1992, p. 26).

Case Two: I had lived in Las Vegas only six months, and we were entertaining our first guests from our old home town—Kalamazoo. It was Joe's first trip to Vegas and he was anxious to get to the Strip and "get it on," as he said. "Where should I go? Which casino?" he pleaded.

I asked, "What do you want to do?"

"Play some slots and maybe some Blackjack," he offered.

"Ok," I replied, "you should go to the Holiday Inn Center Strip casino (it is now Harrah's), and play the one dollar, stand alone, slots. Put in the maximum of three coins—three dollars—on each pull of the handle." I told him to stay away from the progressive machines that offer very enormous jackpots, but very bad odds. I was only repeating the local wisdom that a new resident quickly picks-up upon moving to Las Vegas. The stand alone dollar machines at this one casino purportedly offered the best pay-back odds—over 97%—of any place in town.

Joe told me he had a bankroll of $200. I emphasized to him that he must leave all his credit cards in his suitcase when he went to the Strip. "If you lose it, just quit!" I told him.

Joe went to the Strip at 8 p.m. He returned to my door at midnight. He looked "high." He was "high." His eyes were glazed over, and he was almost jumping up and down. He said (that is, he yelled), "How can you stay at home at night, why aren't you down on the Strip? This is the greatest place on Earth."

I offered that I had a job, I had classes to teach in the morning, and I enjoyed reading and watching the news and Carson on television at night. He shouted, "My God, get your coat on, let's go back to the Strip right now." I offered that I was thinking more about going to sleep. Then he yelled out, "$1200, this is the greatest place on Earth. I won two jackpots, $1200." Again he begged me to go to the Strip. Then he ran to the telephone and began dialing. He said, "Don't worry, I got my telephone card. I gotta call Jack."

I asked, "Jack back in Kalamazoo, Joe! It's 3 a.m. in Michigan."

Joe said that didn't matter. I heard him say, "Jack, I'm in Vegas, this is the greatest place on Earth, I hit two jackpots, $1200. You gotta come to Vegas. Oh? Ok. Bye." Joe hung up the phone.

"Well?" I asked.

Joe said Jack was a little upset being called at 3 a.m. Then he added, "He'll thank me for telling him about Las Vegas." Again he begged me to go down to the Strip.

I said, "O.K. tomorrow we'll go to the Strip, and by the way, why don't you treat us to a show while we're there." (Shows were only $20 back in the early 1980s).

He paused in silence for the first time. He asked, "Why do you think I should take you to a show?" "Well, you do have $1200." He was silent. "Don't you," I asked.

"Oh, well, I put it all back in."

"What about your $200 bankroll?"

"Oh, well, I put that in too."

Joe's behavior is one of the primary reasons that Las Vegas has grown to be the number one overnight tourist destination in the world. In 2000, Las Vegas had 35.8 million visitors, more than even Mecca. Mecca gets 35 million visitors each year, because a Muslim must (if he or she possibly can) make at least one pilgrimage to Mecca in a lifetime, if he or she wishes to get to heaven. Many of the Las Vegas visitors make repeat visits, and I don't think they are making the visits in order to get to a religious heaven.

Las Vegas has succeeded in selling its gambling products through "word of mouth" advertising. As we say in Las Vegas "winners talk and losers walk." With almost any other product—automobiles, appliances, clothing, restaurant meals—those who believe they have received bad results talk. Bad customer stories are repeated. This is not the case with gambling stories. Winners spread the word, and losers stay quiet. It goes even so far as Joe's story. Losers tell stories about their winning experiences and neglect to balance them with stories of the negative bottomline. A winner in Las Vegas is exhilarated, and he or she desires others to offer them congratulations and admiration. Others then see them as worthy and brave. But if a person would tell another that he lost money gambling, the reaction is quite different. From a spouse: "You lost that much gambling! How could you, we need that money for (a) our retirement, (b) our car repairs, (c) the kids' summer camp, (d) the kids' college educations." (pick the poison). A friend might shake his or her head and mumble something about the loser being stupid. A boss might shift his eyes to the cash register and enter a mental note to watch the loser closely. A client or customer might think, "Hum! So that's why the costs are so high." From a macho to a zero. Just one word difference, "I won," "I lost." Losers may indeed be stupid, but they are not so stupid that they let the world know about it.

The Win Win Game – The Mirage

There is a reason gambling is the fastest growing industry in America. More people want to gamble. Why? It is the winning formula. Only with gambling do you hear the winners talking and rarely hear the losers talking (honestly).

Could the industry lose the winning formula? The answer is "yes." There are three problem areas where this could happen.

First, casinos will lose the winning formula if players think they are being cheated. Integrity is a must. The player accepts that the house has a standard edge, but that edge must be reasonable and that edge must not be tampered with.

Second, exploitation can ruin the winning formula.

If casinos seek out the poor as their customer base, there is exploitation.

There is exploitation when drinks are given to a player to cause excessive and unreasonable play. If the player is a known compulsive gambler and the casino allows his losses to mount without intervention, there is exploitation.

Third, bad customer service also can ruin the winning formula. Many casinos operate in near-monopoly situations. They may delude themselves into thinking it is a seller's market and neglect customer service. The winning formula is the backbone of the expanding gambling industry, it must be protected, or it could slip away.

In our customer service book, Michele Comeau and I emphasize the need to keep what we call the "Win-Win game." Casinos will lose this edge on all other businesses if they ever let customers feel that the games are somehow dishonest, or if there is exploitation. But most of all, the edge is lost when the casino does not offer good customer service to players.

Source: William N. Thompson (2001). Customer Service Lecture, Public Administration 736: The Social Impacts of the Gambling Industry, Department of Public Administration, University of Nevada, Las Vegas (Spring); William N. Thompson, "To Keep the Winning Formula," <u>Casino Executive</u>, November, 1955; and William N. Thompson and Michele Comeau. 1992. <u>Casino Customer Service: The WIN-WIN Game</u>. New York City: Gaming and Wagering Business.

Welcome
(Courtesy Special Collections, UNLV)

Chapter 30. An Autobiographical Account of the Las Vegas Welcome Wagon

1980: My little girl said casually: "Did Mom tell you about Kristen?" I said, "No." "Well," she said, "You know, I kinda asked Kristen if she was going to Lisa's Halloween party. When she said, 'No,' I asked her if she had been invited. She said she had been. Then she said, 'I really can't go to parties, because, well, I shouldn't talk about it, but I have like a housekeeper who brings me to school and picks me up. He really isn't a housekeeper. He is a bodyguard. There are some bad people who told my Dad that they are going to get us.'" Kristen's father was the president of a leading casino in Las Vegas.

A couple of years earlier, such a conversation with my daughter would have sent chills up and down my spine. But then I was just another innocent midwesterner, new to Glitter Gulch and the Strip, a neophyte to the tinseltown known as Las Vegas. I have settled in, however. I have a Nevada driver's license, I am registered to vote, and I have had my call for jury duty. I am a native.

As soon as I got my job teaching at the University of Nevada, Las Vegas, I started reading about my new hometown. I hungered for and absorbed the likes of The Green Felt Jungle, The Last Mafioso, Easy Street, The House of Cards, The Girls of Nevada, Hunter Thompson's Fear and Loathing in Las Vegas, Hank Greenspun's Where I Stand, and Ralph Pearl's Las Vegas Is My Beat. I read all the local tourist guides, and I ran to get the paper each morning. I had an insatiable need to know, to learn. The books painted the picture of a quaint desert railroad stop that had been transformed in the 1940s into a haven for gamblers with unsavory reputations elsewhere.

Benjamin "Bugsy" Siegel led the group that sought to operate "legally like" in the small oasis town whose name means "The Meadows." And they settled in. And they "fit in." They founded the country clubs and social clubs. They started the first synagogue and a number of churches, and, of course, private schools. They became good Joe Citizens. They were Joneses next door with whom everyone kept up. The stories were quaint in a menacing sort of way, like a murder mystery on television. But I knew things had to have changed. Las Vegas had grown into a metropolis. I was sure that the older professors would be able to tell me stories about the unsavory characters I had been reading about. And I did thrill at the stories that real natives-who can actually be found-told me. But, for me, the characters would be just names in the papers or names in the local history books. So I thought.

For my first few months in Vegas, the papers didn't give too much attention to its notorious inhabitants. They had other stories to report. The MGM fire took eighty-four lives, the Hilton fire eight more. These tragedies had hit corporate casinos, not mob hangouts. No unsavory characters, just "good ole" American enterprise, corporations after a quick buck, willing to cut corners on building codes in order to get their profits a little faster. Las Vegas seemed more typical every day.

The first hot gaming story involving the city's "new solid citizen" types concerned Andy "The Ant" Contralto. The local press introduced me to the famous Nevada Black Book, the official list of unacceptable characters who were not permitted on the premises of any of the 216 establishments that held Nevada gaming licenses. Contralto, allegedly the contact man in Las Vegas for the Chicago mob, took some friends out to dinner at Diamond Lil's Restaurant in Sam's Town Casino. The police were tipped off and swooped in for the catch. But as they arrived, Contralto drove off. He was later found innocent of the Black Book violation after claiming that the person at Sam's Town had really been his brother. Witnesses could not positively establish his presence there. Andy has two brothers in Las Vegas, Bobby and Fred. I first heard about Fred in the papers too. In 1981, he was sentenced to seven months in federal prison for income tax evasion. My little girl also brought the story home from school. She told me that her friend's father was going to have to go to jail.

Gunshots were fired into the homes of Bobby and Fred later in the year. The parents of another of my daughter's friends told us how they wouldn't let their little girl play at Shirley Marie's house any more. They were just afraid of what might happen there. A few months later, all the girls spent the night at Shirley Marie's birthday slumber party. There really wasn't anything to fear, and the girls could not get over just how nice Shirley Marie's parents were.

We knew that they must have brought their kids up right. On Awards Night at Orr Junior High, their little girl trotted up to the stage time after time to accept this academic award and that citizenship award. Nevada's attorney general, Richard Bryan, later governor of the state, and then a U.S. senator, presided at the honors ceremony. I wondered if a stray thought or two about organized crime was running through his mind as he heard the name "Contralto" repeated over and over.

Probably not. He has been a native almost all his life.

That first Vegas summer, we sent our daughter back to the Midwest to be with her grandparents and old friends. It was a time of great happiness for her. She had not adjusted well to Las Vegas. But the departure did have one sour note. Her friend Laurie was upset because her father disappeared. The kids at school were sort of worried over Laurie.

We kept the news from our daughter over the summer, but she found out when she came back in the fall. The father-a wonderful family man who really loved his children-had been "wasted" gangland style. His head was found by a dog in the desert near Needles, California. Laurie is doing well now. She is a good student. I took the girls to the high school football game a few weekends ago. They seemed to have a good time.

The start of summer 1981 also brought our introduction to the Paradise Valley Little League. First came the tryouts. Would our boy make the majors or be sent to the minors? It's a Little League parent's nightmare. The non-native parents did a double take as the loud speaker read the names of the players making the tryouts. Little Andrew Contralto stepped to the plate. It didn't matter how well he did—in fact, he got a decent hit—when it was announced that he was coach's choice for a major league team. He was Fred's boy.

My kid made the minors. In fact, they had to expand the league to make room for him and other kids. His expansion team was sponsored by Rumba Pools. They were a quickly arranged expansion team, and the league officials grabbed anyone who wanted to coach. The Rumba coach was an unkept young man of about twenty, with shabby clothes and totally unwashed, unshaven face. He seemed friendly, so the parents thought it was probably OK. But we certainly became apprehensive when he was delivered, always late, to games and practices by grubby friends in junky-looking "low rider" cars. His younger brother was assigned to the team, and somehow this kid became the permanent pitcher. His stepmother became the team mother, but as they didn't have an address or phone, no one knew where to call to remind them that they had called a practice or that there was a game scheduled. When they did get to the games, things were worse. They couldn't keep the kid's names straight, lineups were constantly messed up, and several kids wouldn't get into the games, in violation of league rules. Many parents, myself included, were especially angry over this latter fact.

The anger peaked when the coach appeared at a game stoned. The time to speak out had arrived. I reluctantly called Tommy Gazela, the league's vice president, and asked if my kid could be on another team. He asked me if the problem I had was with the Rumba Bears. I said it was. He relayed the fact that I was not the first to call; I was the last. I had actually been the most patient of the parents. I wasn't yet a full-fledged native. The league officials called a meeting of all the parents. For some reason or another, one parent, Peggy, wanted me to be a critic. When I showed up at the meeting, she was delighted. She later told me that my presence had made all the difference, that the other parents knew that if the cool-headed professor was concerned, action had to be taken. I protested that I had kept my mouth shut at the meeting. She reiterated that my silence made my presence even more meaningful. But I had kept my mouth shut because I didn't want anyone to think anything about me at all. I was there only because Peggy had leaned on me. At the meeting, I remember nudging Peggy and saying, "Who is that presiding?" She said, "Oh, that's Bobby." I said, "Bobby?" She put her finger up to her mouth, and uttered a noticeable "Shhhh!" The she whispered, "Bobby Contralto. He's the league president." I whispered, "Who is sitting next to Tommy Gazela taking notes?" Peggy whispered, "That's Tommy's wife. She is the league secretary." I said quietly and with a chuckle: "At least the mob didn't elect all the league officers." She laughed and whispered, "She's Bobby's sister." "Oh," I replied. And I determined, once again, to keep my mouth shut.

The more vocal parents let their tirades fly, and the coach hadn't bothered to show up to defend himself. So, bowing to the pressures of the crowd, the league officials agreed to replace him with one of the parents, who was quite willing to tackle the job. "We took on the Mob and we won," I thought. "And we lived to tell about it." At the next game, Gazela and Brother Bobby went around to all the parents almost apologetically, saying, "Hey, yeah, everything is OK." Peggy kept telling me that I had made the difference. "No way, Peggy. No way, Tommy. No way, Bobby." But then, the FBI just may be reviewing my telephone conversation with the Little League vice president today.

John Moran was elected sheriff of Clark County and chief of the Metropolitan Police Force in 1982. During the campaign, he was accused of taking political contributions from Andy "The Ant." He was also accused of associating with low-life mob types, among them Vince Rubano, who had been the emcee of a fund-raising rally and barbecue for the candidate. Indignantly, Moran denied the charges and took a lie detector test to prove his innocence. The Moran forces were up in arms about their opponents defaming Rubano, a well-liked local philanthropist. I wondered.

A few weeks later, a nice-looking car pulled up to my house to drop off my little girl after school. The car had personalized Nevada license plates reading RUMBA. I asked her, "RUMBA?" She said, "Yes, my friend's father owns Rumba Pools. I said, "What's his name?" "Oh, that's Mr. Rubano." Follow-up stories in the press indicated that this Little League team sponsor had quite a long FBI file. Just friends and neighbors.

How friendly, how neighborly? I wondered as I pulled into the drive one Saturday night about 1 A.M., just wanting get into the house and get some sleep before church. "What is that?" My wife said. I looked and there was a man standing beside a car right in front of our house. "I don't know, but let's get into the house," I responded. Watching the man apparently talking to someone in the car, I grew more concerned. He looked big and ugly. I kept peeping out the window. I did feel a little better when I saw a police car pass by, but it would have been nicer if the police car had stopped. It didn't. The man stayed there. Then there was a loud knock at my door. "What the hell is this?" I thought. "Yeah," I yelled through the door. "Police," the man said. I said, "Go to the window." He did, and he showed me a badge. He said he could tell that I was concerned, and he just wanted to me to know he was going to be there all night, and it didn't have anything to do with me. I took him at his word.

On Friday night I had gone to Safeway for some milk at about 8:30. The Saturday news reported that a man had been abducted from the parking lot next to Safeway at 9 P.M. Friday and taken to Sunrise Mountain, where his body was found, "done-in mob style." The Sunday Las Vegas Review-Journal told the rest of the story. The poor fellow was a house guest of Moe Valzano's. The two were spending Friday with some friends at Moe's house, and they decided to have some ice cream. The guest went out to get it in Moe's fancy car, but he didn't come home. The police speculated that the abductors were after Valzano and had been watching his house. They grabbed his guest by mistake. The paper went on about how Valzano was a past partner of Sal Albino, Laurie's father, in the Crazy Pony Saloon and was in a struggle with the Chicago mob over control of topless joints and porno bookstores in Los Angeles and Las Vegas.

All during that Saturday night-with the police watch in my front yard-I was awake, wondering which of my neighbors was in trouble. Could it have been the neighbor who had had an accident and was facing over $30,000 in hospital bills? Could he have robbed a bank? Perhaps it was the neighbor who owned Cicero Al's restaurant, a name that would seem to invite trouble? The twenty-one dealer who had just gotten a divorce? Maybe the settlement hadn't been all amicable. Or maybe the trouble came from the empty house that had been head-quarters of the rock band. All night I worried and wondered. The Sunday paper relieved me of my suspicious about my immediate neighbors, all except one. The paper gave Moe Valzano's address. He lived next door to the residence directly behind my own. He lived on my block. The stakeout was protective. The police wanted to be sure that the murderers of Moe's house guest didn't come back to try again.

Neighbor Moe is now trying to sell his house. He doesn't need it. He has another home, Terminal Island Federal Prison. Moe gladly pleaded guilty to minor drug charges in exchange for joining the federal witness protection program. If he survives, he is expected to live to testify about the activities of Andy "the Ant" and his friends. Moe won't be seen at the local Safeway for a long time.

The case of Valzano and the mistaken identity problem worries me. But I am a native, and I am sure I shall adjust. In the meanwhile, I'll keep driving my Toyota Corolla, thank you. Just a safety measure.

I tell all my unemployed friends in the Midwest to come out to Vegas. It sure is a neat place to be: good schools, lots of churches, good concerts, good parks, fabulous weather, and nice scenery. Any native can tell you Las Vegas is a good family town.

*Pp. 208-213 ("How I Became a Native," by William N. Thompson) in Hal Rothman and Mike Davis, 2001 eds. The Grit

William N. Thompson

<u>Beneath the Glitter: Tales from the Real Las Vegas</u>. Berkeley: University of California Press, 2002. By Permission.

Selected Writings by The Author

Books

Over the Top: Solutions to the Sisyphus Dilemmas of Life. Bloomington, IN: 1st Books Library, 2003. 158 pp. With Bradley L. Kenny.

Gambling in America: An Encyclopedia. Santa Barbara, CA; Denver, C0; and Oxford, England: ABC-Clio, 2001. 531 pp.

International Casino Law. Reno: Institute for the Study of Gambling, University of Nevada, Reno, 1999, Third Edition. 650 pp. With Anthony Cabot, Andrew Tottenham, and Carl Braunlich. (1st Edition, 1991; 2nd Edition, 1993).

Legalized Gambling: A Reference Handbook. Santa Barbara, CA; Denver, CO; and Oxford, England: ABC-Clio, 1997 2nd Edition. 295 pp. (1st Edition, 1994).

Native American Issues: A Reference Handbook. Santa Barbara, CA; Denver, CO; and Oxford, England: ABC-Clio, 1996. 280 pp.

Casino Customer Service = The Win-Win Game. New York City: Gaming and Wagering Business, 1992 and 1997, 350 pp. With Michele Comeau.

The Last Resort: Success and Failure in Campaigns for Casinos. Reno: University of Nevada Press, 1990. 220 pp. With John Dombrink.

State Attorneys General and The Environment. Kalamazoo, MI: New Issues Press, Western Michigan University, 1974 and 1975. 95 pp. With Bradley F. Smith.

Monographs

Not Exactly "A Fair Share": Revenue Sharing and Native American Casinos in Wisconsin. Wisconsin Policy Research Institute. February 2002. With Robert Schmidt.

A Study Concerning the Effects of Legalized Gambling on the Citizens of the State of Connecticut. Prepared for State of Connecticut, Department of Revenue Services. June 1997. With Henry Lesieur, ICR Survey Research Group, and staff of WEFA Group.

The Economic Impact of the Arts in Chicago. Better Government Association of Chicago. June 1997. With Ricardo Gazel.

Casinos and Crime in Wisconsin: What's the Connection. Wisconsin Policy Research Institute. November 1996. with Ricardo Gazel and Dan Rickman.

The Economics of Casino Gambling in Illinois. Better Government Association of Chicago. July 1996. With Ricardo Gazel.

The Social Costs of Gambling in Wisconsin. Wisconsin Policy Research Institute. July 1996. With Ricardo Gazel and Dan Rickman.

The Economic Impact of Native American Gaming in Wisconsin. Wisconsin Policy Research Institute. April 1995. With Ricardo Gazel and Dan Rickman.

The Office of Attorney General. National Association of Attorneys General. 1971. Authored chapters on administration of departments of justice, environmental protection, riots and civil disorder, and state structures for providing legal services.

Articles

"How I Became a Native," in <u>The Grit Beneath the Glitter: Tales from the Real Las Vegas</u>, Hal Rothman and Mike Davis, eds. Berkeley: University of California Press, 2002. Pp. 208-213.

"Nevada Goes Global: The Foreign Gaming Rule and the Spread of Casinos," in <u>The Grit Beneath the Glitter: Tales from the Real Las Vegas</u>, Hal Rothman and Mike Davis, eds. Berkeley: University of California Press, 2002. Pp. 347-362.

"Political Cultures and Gambling: Two Recent Case Studies. (Victoria, Australia and New York State)." <u>Gaming Law Review</u>, v. 6, 2002, pp. 431-437.

"I'm Moving On: Reflections upon the Career of the 'Singing Ranger' Clarence Eugene 'Hank' Snow." <u>Popular Culture Review</u>, v. 12, 2002, pp. 135-146. With Michael Green.

"Policy Making for Nevada Gaming," Chapter 8 in <u>Nevada in the New Millenium</u>, Eric Herzik, Dennis Soden, and Royse Smith, eds. Dubuque: Kendall/Hunt, 2001. Pp. 143-160.

"Gambling in Israel and the Jericho Casino: Moralistic Political Culture Bends Toward Pragmaticism," <u>Gaming Law Review</u>, v. 3, 2001, pp. 25-32. With Asher Friedberg and Carl Lutrin.

"Tom T. Hall and Critical Junctions in Country Music," <u>Popular Culture Review</u>, v. 10, 1999, pp. 139-147.

"The South Carolina Battlefield," <u>Gaming Law Review</u>, v. 3, 1999, pp. 5-8.

"Steve Wynn: I Got the Message." a chapter in <u>Maverick Spirit: Profiles of Nevada Leaders</u>, Richard Davis, ed. Reno: University of Nevada Press, 1998. Pp. 194-210.

"Casinos de Juegos del Mundo: A Survey of World Gaming," The Annals of the American Academy of Political Science, in Special Issue on Gambling, v.556, 1998, pp. 11-20. James Frey, editor.

"The Family that Gambles Together: Business and Social Concerns," Journal of Travel Research, 1996, pp. 70-75. With J. Kent Pinney and Jack Schibrowsky.

"The States Bet on Legalized Gambling," The 1994 World Book Year Book, World Book, Inc, 1994, pp. 391-401.

"Not in My Backyard: Las Vegas Residents Protest Casinos," Journal of Gambling Studies, v.9, 1993, pp. 47-62. With R. Keith Schwer, Richard Hoyt, and Dolores Brosnan.

"Machismo: Manifestations of A Cultural Value in the Latin American Casino," Journal of Gambling Studies, v. 7, 1991, pp. 143-164.

"Fishermen of the Tittabawassee: Environmental Sociology," Environment, v. 26, 1984, pp. 5, 43. With Bradley Smith.

"The Office of the Attorney General of Nevada in the Nineteenth Century, Part II," Nevada Historical Society Quarterly, 1984, pp.13-39.

"The Office of the Attorney General of Nevada in the Nineteenth Century, Part I,"Nevada Historical Society Quarterly, 1983, pp.272-97.

"Public Pension Plans:The Need for Scrutiny and Control, "Public Personnel Management, v.6, 1977, pp. 203-224.

"Conflicts of Interest and State Attorneys General," Washburn University Law Journal, v. 15, 1975, pp.15-39. With Lee Gough and John Wallace.

The Author

Courtesy Diana Sjoberg

William N. Thompson, a native of Ann Arbor, Michigan, is a Professor of Public Administration at the University of Nevada, Las Vegas (UNLV). He joined the faculty of UNLV in 1980, after serving on faculties of Southeast Missouri State and Western Michigan Universities. While on a sabbatical leave in 1986-1987 he studied casino gambling throughout Europe and also taught with the Troy State University European Division. His Bachelors and Masters degrees in Political Science were awarded by Michigan State University, and he earned his Ph.D., also in Political Science, from the University of Missouri in Columbia. He held a Public Administration fellowship and worked with the Pension Administration in the United States Department of Labor, and he also was a candidate for the Michigan legislature, and he held the elective post of Supervisor (chief administrator) of Kalamazoo Charter Township in Michigan. His areas of study have included state constitutional reform, and public policy with emphasis on the environment, public pension reform, and gambling. He served as a research associate with the National Association of Attorneys General and wrote his doctoral dissertation on the political ambitions of state attorneys general. He lives in Las Vegas with Kay, his wife of 38 years. They have a daughter and two sons.

www.ingramcontent.com/pod-product-compliance
Lightning Source LLC
Chambersburg PA
CBHW051438280526
45785CB00003B/1334